Connections

Beginning
Student Edition

Suzanne Carter * Dorothy Woods

English Anywhere Inc.
6513 Patricia Avenue
Plano, Texas 75023

www.englishanywhere.org

copyright 2009
Printed in the United States of America

ISBN-13: 978-1517005900

ISBN-10: 1517005906

Acknowledgements

As the need for speaking English becomes a world wide necessity, the teachers of English are faced with many choices for good curriculum. These lessons are the basic knowledge that students need to begin their acquisition of the English language. Our goal is to provide a structured textbook that can be used by teachers and students to accomplish the skills necessary to speak English as a native speaker. The lessons are designed to aid the student in the spoken language and assume that they have already mastered some of the reading and writing skills taught in many schools around the world.

We have incorporated the most current teaching techniques for acquiring a language, and use many activities to aid in practicing the skills taught in each lesson. In Lesson 12 we included a story and use Penny Hiller's Story Approach to teach the skills needed in that lesson. We have employed the basic concepts of Gardner's *Theory of Multiple Intelligences* to reach the widest range of student's learning, and we hope you will enjoy teaching these lessons.

Special thanks to:

Gloria Ormiston for field testing these lessons in Enable Learning Center in Minneapolis, Minnesota and in the church in Bangkok, Thailand.

Ed Woods for the many hours of contributions and help with these lessons at Enable Learning Center in Minneapolis, Minnesota.

Frank Fitzgerald for helping in the ESL classes at Southern Hills Baptist Church, Tulsa, Oklahoma.

Charles and Yoke Fong Harvey for the support of Grace Ministries and the encouragement they gave as we taught the lessons in Krasang, Thailand.

All of our friends and families who have given their financial, prayer, and spiritual support throughtout the long process of writing and field testing this curriculum.

About the Authors

Suzanne Carter (Texas)

Suzanne is founder and director of English Anywhere, and is retired from teaching elementary school for 33 years. She has been teaching English as Second Language (ESL) for the past 16 years in the USA and in many foreign countries. She has also trained many church volunteers and missionaries to teach ESL curriculum as they seek to serve in their communities. She earned her Bachelor of Science in Education degree from the University of Tulsa, and she got her TESOL certification from Oxford Seminars. She has one daughter. She is currently teaching 4 ESL classes in Texas and training TESOL at the Graduate Institute of Applied Linguistics in Dallas.

Dorothy A. Woods (New York)

Dorothy has served alongside her husband, Edward, as church planters with Continental Baptist Missions since 1970. She has a graduate degree in education and a wide variety of teaching experience. Since 1994, the Lord has privileged Ed and Dorothy to focus on ESL (English as a Second Language) as an outreach of the local church. They have conducted tutor training workshops in churches and Bible colleges in the US, Canada, and overseas. Currently the Woods are living in Minneapolis, where they teach ESL through the Enable Learning Center to Hmong refugees, assist international students at the University of Minnesota, and continue to challenge and equip Christians for Great Commission living. The Woods have three grown children and three grandsons.

Illustrations:

Victor Zamora (Mexico)

Victor is Academic Director for Instituto Blas Pascal. He has taught English for over 12 years to children and adults. He illustrated the Good Neighbor story in Lesson 11.

Cover designed by:

Cynthia Reed (Oklahoma)

Cynthia is the graphics designer and owner of Cynpro Professional Solutions.

Overview

Connections is a conversational English curriculum with an overview of the Bible. It is designed to be used in long term classes lasting 9 months or longer. The format is conversation driven, and it is created to get students speaking from the first lesson. This is a whole language approach working from conversations to break down various sentences, phrases and sound studied in each lesson. The lessons start with a **Theme Picture** to discover any preknowledge students have and set the tone of the lesson. Then the **Conversations** are taught with the vocabulary being taught in the context of the conversations. Next we work on specific sounds and the rhythms of the of the English language in the **Pronunciation** and **Rhythm** segments. Finally, there is a section that discusses a **Bible** lesson. There are 2 parts to each lesson and many activities to give diversity to the English practice.

Recommended books for the lessons are:

A Look Inside America
by Bill Perry
ISBN 0-9633645-5-3

Word by Word Basic Picture Dictionary
by Steven J. Molinsky and Bill Bliss
ISBN 0-13-200355-4

Recommended videos:
"The Hope"
by Mars Hill Productions Inc.
Mars-Hill.org
ISBN 1-892271-02-8

"The God Story"
Produced by the Jeremiah Team
god-story.org

Table of Contents

Introduction

Creation

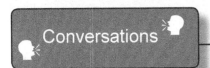

Conversations

Part 1

A. <u>Hi.</u> How are you?
B. <u>Fine,</u> thank you. And you?
A. <u>Fine.</u> Thank you.

hello
hi

Part 2

A. Hello, my name is <u>Mary</u>. What's your name?
B. My name is <u>Jim</u>. It's nice to meet you.
A. It's nice to meet you, too.

Hello, my name is <u>Susie</u>. What's your name?

My name is <u>Linda Smith</u>. It's nice to meet you.

It's nice to meet you, too.

I am _____
I'm _____ .

Present tense am - is - are

Singular	Contractions	Examples:
I am	I am - I'm	I'm <u>Susan.</u>
you are	he is - he's	He's <u>fine.</u>
he/she is	she is - she's	She's <u>happy</u>.
it is	it is - it's	It's <u>good</u>.
Plural		
you are	you are - you're	You're <u>sad</u>.
we are	we are - we're	We're <u>unhappy.</u>
they are	they are - they're	They're <u>fine</u>.

sad
unhappy

fine
happy
good

Song:

He's Got the Whole World in His Hands

He's got the whole world in His hands.
He's got the whole world in His hands.
He's got the whole world in His hands.
He's got the whole world in His hands.

He = God

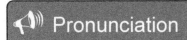

Pronunciation

* The asterisk indicates the words for Part 2

h
hi
hello
how
he's
his
hands
*heavens

n
name
nice
in
and
hands
*beginning
*heavens

long e
me
meet
he
he's
*created
*beginning

Rhythm

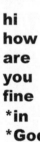

●
hi
how
are
you
fine
*in
*God
*and
*earth

●
thank
and
my
name
is
*he's
*got
*the
*whole
*world

●
it's
nice
to
meet
*his
*hands
*I'm
*what's
*your
*name

In the beginning
God created the heavens and the earth.
Genesis 1:1

Definitions:
In the beginning God created the heavens and the earth.

beginning--the first part, start

God--the Creator

created-- past tense of *create*; to make something

heavens--sky and clouds, sun, moon, stars, and planets,

earth - continents and oceans

Grammar: verbs

Present tense Singular	Past tense Singular
I create	I created
you create	you created
he creates	he created
she creates	she created
it creates	it created
Plural	**Plural**
we create	we created
you create	you created
they create	they created

1 Beginnings

God
and
Creation

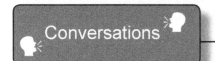
Part 1

A. What's your phone number?
B. My phone number is _____.
   It's ___.

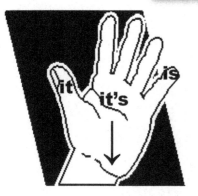

Grammar:
what's = what is
what - a question word
it's = it is
it = a pronoun

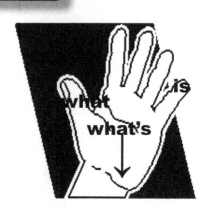

Part 2

A. What's your address?
B. My address is _____.
      It's ___.

5660 Elm Street

Numbers:

0 - zero	
1 - one	*
2 - two	**
3 - three	***
4 - four	****
5 - five	*****
6 - six	******
7 - seven	*******
8 - eight	********
9 - nine	*********

1-	918-	234-5678
country code	area code	phone number

Address:

a street - St.
an avenue - Ave.
a place - Pl.
a drive - Dr.
a post office box
 - PO Box
Teach:
local city, state,
country, zip code
or postal numbers

an apartment
a house
a mobile home

678 Pine Dr. Apt. 4
City, State 09876

Jane Doe
1234 Oak Ave.
City, State 12345

John Doe
PO Box 123
City, State 12345

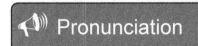
* Asterisks indicate Part 2 words.

f	m	s	long **i**
fine	**m**y	**s**ix	hi
four	I'**m**	**s**even	f**i**ve
five	**m**eet	**s**ad	n**i**ne
***f**ish	***m**oon	***s**eas	n**i**ce
***f**alse	*na**m**e	***s**un	*l**i**fe
***ph**one	*nu**m**ber		*l**i**ght

Rhythm

phone
one
two
three
four
five
six
eight
nine

he's
got
the
whole
world
in
his
hands
***God**
***was**
***good**

thank you
address
number
happy
zero
seven
***heav**ens
***coun**try
***wa**ter

Song:

He = God

1. He's Got the Whole World in His Hands

He's got the whole world in His hands.
He's got the whole world in His hands.
He's got the whole world in His hands.
He's got the whole world in His hands.

More verses:

2. He's got <u>the heaven and earth</u> in His hands.
   He's got <u>the light and the dark</u> in His hands.
   He's got <u>the sky and the land</u> in His hands.
   He's got the whole world in His hands.
3. He's got <u>the seas and the plants</u> in His hands.
   He's got <u>the sun, moon, and stars</u> in His hands.
   He's got <u>the animals and man</u> in His hands.
   He's got the whole world in His hands.
4. On the seventh day He rested from all His work.(sing 3X)
   He's got the whole world in His hands.

17

Bible
Lesson

Part 1

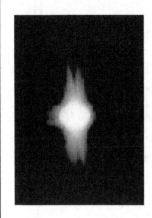  

God created light and dark. He made the sky and water. He made the land and seas. Everything was good.

Taken from Genesis 1

Discussion Questions
1. What did God create?
2. What did God make?
3. How was everything?

Opposites:

| 1 + 1 = 2 true   yes |
| 1 + 1 = 3 false   no |

| light |
| dark |

good   bad

life   death

Definitions:
God created light and dark.
  God - the all-powerful being
  created - made
  light and dark - day and night
He made the sky and water.
  He = God.
  sky - the air
  water - H2O, solid, liquid, gas
He made the land and seas.
  land - ground
  seas - salt water
Everything was good.
  everything - all things.
  was - past tense of *is*
  good - best (opposite - bad)

Part 2

He made the trees and plants;
sun, moon, and stars;
birds and fish,
and animals and man.
Everything was good.
There was no death.

Genesis 1

Definitions:

He made the trees and plants;
sun, moon, and stars; birds and fish;
animals and man.
He = God
made - past tense of *make.*
trees, plants, sun, moon, stars, birds, fish, animals, man
Everything was good.
Everything - all
was - past tense of *to be*
There was no death.
no - none, zero
death - no life, no movement

Discussion Questions
1. What did God make?
2. How was everything?
3. What wasn't there?

Grammar: verbs

Present tense Singular	Past tense Singular
I make	I made
you make	you made
he makes	he made
she makes	she made
it makes	it made
Plural	Plural
we make	we made
you make	you made
they make	they made

Present tense singular	Past tense singular
I am	I was
you are	you were
he is	he was
she is	she was
it is	it was
Plural	Plural
we are	we were
you are	you were
they are	they were

2   Family

The First Family

Conversations

Part 1

A. What is this?
B. This is <u>a family</u>.
A. Who is this?
B. This is <u>a mother.</u>

A. John, this is my family.

B. Who are these people?
A. They're my <u>brothers</u>.

B. Who is this person?
A. He is my <u>son</u>.

B. Who is that person?
A. She is my <u>sister</u>.

Part 2

A. I'm <u>a mother</u>.
B. I'm <u>a father</u>.

A. This is my <u>family.</u>
B. Who is this?
A. This is my <u>mother</u>. Her name is ___.
That is my <u>father</u>. His name is ___.
These are my <u>children</u>. Their names are ___.
   (Repeat these sentences putting in the right
   family members and names.)

He / his is the pronoun for a male.
She / her is the pronoun for a female.

What is this? This is a _____.
What are these? These are _____.

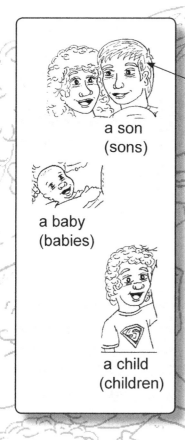

a son
(sons)

a baby
(babies)

a child
(children)

a father   a mother
(fathers)   (mothers)
dad   mom

a wife   a husband
(wives)   (husbands)

a daughter
(daughters)

a brother
(brothers)

a sister
(sisters)

Grammar:
Verb: to have
Present tense

Singular
I have
you have
he has
she has
it has

Plural
we have
you have
they have

A.   How many _____ do you have?
B.   I have 2 children.

1, 2, 3, 4, 5, 6, 7, 8, 9, 10,

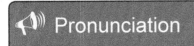
th
the
this
these
***th**at
***th**ose
*fa**th**er
*mo**th**er
*bro**th**er

short a
and
h**a**nds
animals
pl**a**nts
*m**a**n
*f**a**mily
*b**a**d

w
was
world
woman
women
***w**ife
***w**ives

short e
everything
th**e**m
addr**e**ss
*m**e**n
*wom**e**n
*h**e**av**e**n

Rhythm ♫

●

son
wife
child
how
have
who
***kid**
***see**
***saw**

●

trees
plants
sun
moon
stars
birds
***fish**
***man**
***there**
***was**
***no**
***death**

● ○

father
mother
baby
brother
sister
***daugh**ter
***chil**dren
***hus**band
***wo**man

* Asterisks indicate words for Part 2

Idiom/Slang:

a friend (friends)
a pal (pals)
a buddy (buddies)

a kid = a child, a
    young person
kids = children or
    young people
mom = mother
dad = father

Song:

He = God

He's Got the Whole World in His Hands

He's got the whole world in His hands.
He's got the whole world in His hands.
He's got the whole world in His hands.
He's got the whole world in His hands.

Verse 2:   He's got the <u>fathers</u> and the <u>mothers</u> in His hands.
             He's got the <u>fathers</u> and the <u>mothers</u> in His hands.
             He's got the <u>fathers</u> and the <u>mothers</u> in His hands.
             He's got the whole world in His hands.

Verse 3:   He's got the <u>sons</u> and the <u>daughters</u> in His hands.
Verse 4:   He's got the <u>sisters</u> and the <u>brothers</u> in His hands.
Verse 5:   He's got the <u>babies</u> and the <u>children</u> in His hands.
Verse 6:   He's got the <u>husbands</u> and the <u>wives</u> in His hands.

Chant:

This, That,
These, Those,
Snap your fingers.
Touch your toes

Bible
Lesson

Part 1

God created a man and a woman and told them to have a family. He saw everything that He created.   It was good. There was no death.

Definitions:

God created a man and a woman and told them to have a family.

a man - a male

a woman - a female

told-- Past tense of *to tell.* Example: I <u>tell</u> my children to be good.

I <u>told</u> my children to be good, yesterday.

them-- plural for people

to have - Examples: I <u>have</u> a mother. I <u>have</u> a father.

family - mother, father, children

He saw everthing he created.

He = God

saw -- Past tense of *to see.* Example: I <u>see</u> a man. I <u>see</u> a woman.

I <u>saw</u> a man yesterday.

everything-- all

It was good.

it - all of creation

was - Past tense of *to be*

good - best, opposite of *bad*

There was no death.

no - Review Opposites: yes-no

death - dead, not alive;   Opposites: life- death, alive-dead

Discussion Questions:
1. Who created a man and a woman?
2. What did God tell them?
3. Who saw everything?
4. What did God see?
5. What was it like?
6. What wasn't there?

Part 2

a woman   a man

Grammar: verbs

Present tense Singular	Past tense\ Singular
I tell	I told
you tell	you told
he tells	he told
she tells	she told
it tells	it told
Plural	**Plural**
we tell	we told
you tell	you told
they tell	they told

Present tense singular	Past tense singular
I see	I saw
you see	you saw
he sees	he saw
she sees	she saw
it sees	it saw
Plural	**Plural**
we see	we saw
you see	you saw
they see	they saw

Opposites

good- something that is best for you

bad- something that is not best

3   The World

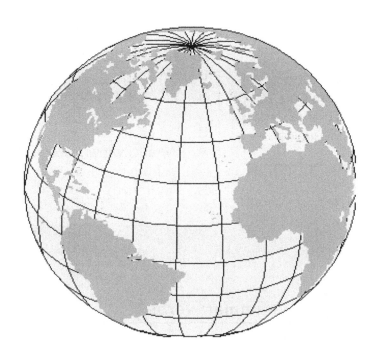

The Beginning of Sin

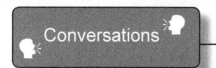
Part 1

A. Where do you live?
B. I live at address .
A. What is your phone number?
B. My phone number is _____.

Prepositions:
from - out of
at - a place
in - inside

A. What country are you from?
B. I'm from _____.
A. What state/province are you from?
B. I'm from _____.
A. What city/town/village are you from?
B. I'm from _____.

Grammar: verbs

Present		Past	
I	live	I	lived
you	live	you	lived
he	lives	he	lived
she	lives	she	lived
it	lives	it	lived
we	live	we	lived
they	live	they	lived

Examples:

Present tense
I live at 5660 Elm Street .
You live in North America.
He lives at 123 Adams Avenue.
She lives in Asia.
It lives in the village.
We live in South America.
They live in Europe.

Past tense
I lived at 5660 Elm Street.
You lived in North America.
He lived at 123 Adams Avenue.
She lived in Asia.
It lived in the country.
We lived in South America.
They lived in Europe.

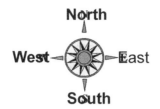

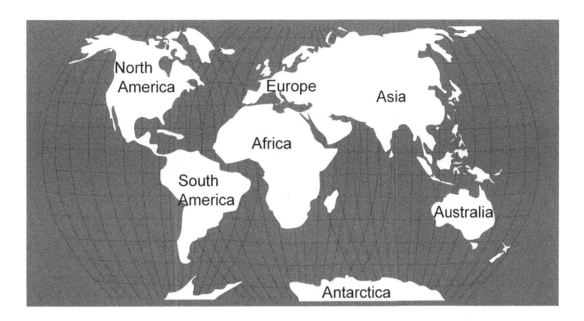

Grammar: verbs

Present		Past	
I	come	I	came
you	come	you	came
he	comes	he	came
she	comes	she	came
it	comes	it	came
we	come	we	came
they	come	they	came

Geography words:

continent(s)
country (countries)
state(s)
province(s)
city (cities)
town(s)
village(s)

Examples:

Present tense
I come from North America .
You come from South America.
He comes from Asia.
She comes from Africa.
It comes from Antarctica.
We come from Europe.
They come from Australia.

Past tense
I came from North America.
You came from South America.
He came from Asia.
She came from Africa.
It came from Antarctica.
We came from Europe.
They came from Australia.

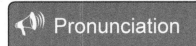
d	**c (k)**	**th**	**short i**
do	**c**ontinent	**Th**ursday	**d**id
did	**c**ountry	ear**th**	live
day	**c**reated	nor**th**	city
dark	**c**ode	sou**th**	**vil**lage
daughter	***c**ome	*dea**th**	*sin
***d**eath	***c**ame	*thing	*be**gin**ning
***D**eliverer			*minutes
***D**ecember			

 Rhythm

●	●○	●○○
north	**ad**dress	**con**tinents
south	**num**ber	**prov**inces
east	**A**sia	**vil**lages
west	**coun**try	**Af**rica
from	**vil**lage	**ev**erything
at	**pro**vince	***Sat**urday
state	***A**dam	***af**ternoon
town	***pro**mised	***yes**terday
*Eve	*al**so**	
*send	*Gar**den**	
*leave	*Ed**en**	
*made	*morn**ing**	
*watch	*eve**ning**	
*clock		

Part 1

The Beginning of Sin

Adam and Eve did not obey God.
This was the beginning of sin and death.
God promised to send the Deliverer.
God also made Adam and Eve leave the Garden of Eden.

Taken from Genesis 3

Definitions:

Adam and Eve did not obey God.

did - past tense of *to do*;

Present tense: I do obey God.
Past tense: I did obey God.

not - no, negative

obey - to do what someone tells you to do;

This was the beginning of sin and death.

was - past of *be*

sin - to do or think something against God

death - to die, not breathing

God promised to send a Deliverer.

promised - pledged, past tense of *promise*

to send - to give something; to give a gift

the Deliverer - one who delivers, the Savior, the Christ, Jesus

God also made Adam and Eve leave the Garden of Eden.

also - to add

Adam - the first man

Eve - the first woman

leave - go away, present tense of *leave*

Garden of Eden - a special perfect garden

Grammar: verbs

Present	Past
I do	I did
you do	you did
he does	he did
she does	she did
it does	it did
we do	we did
they do	they did

Grammar: verbs

Present	Past
I obey	I obeyed
you obey	you obeyed
he obeys	he obeyed
she obeys	she obeyed
it obeys	it obeyed
we obey	we obeyed
they obey	they obeyed

Discussion Questions:
1. Who did not obey God?
2. What was beginning?
3. Who did God promise to send?
4. What did God make Adam & Eve do?
5. Why did Adam and Eve die?
6. What did Adam and Eve have to do?
7. Why did God make Adam and Eve leave the Garden?

Part 2

Opposites:

life   death

Grammar: verbs

Present		Past	
I	promise	I	promised
you	promise	you	promised
he	promises	he	promised
she	promises	she	promised
it	promises	it	promised
we	promise	we	promised
they	promise	they	promised

Note:
It is not used very
often with promises.

Examples:

Present tense
I promise to obey God.
Do you promise to pick me up?
He promises to call at 6:00.
She promises to come home at 10:00.
We promise to obey our parents.
They promise to leave at 8:00.

Past tense
I promised to obey God.
You promised to pick me up.
He promised to call at 6:00.
She promised to come home at 10:00.
We promised to obey our parents.
They promised to leave at 8:00.

Note:
You is the same;
singular or plural.

Grammar: verbs

Present		Past	
I	leave	I	left
you	leave	you	left
he	leaves	he	left
she	leaves	she	left
it	leaves	it	left
we	leave	we	left
they	leave	they	left

Examples:

I left the city.
You must leave the country.
He left the garden.
She leaves the village to see her father.
We leave the village on Monday.
They left the Garden of Eden.

Part 2

a watch
(watches)

Time
hours: minutes
3 : 00
Three o'clock

a digital clock

Polite Expressions:
* excuse me
* thank you very much
* you're welcome

A. Excuse me, what time is it?
B. It's 12:05.
A. Thank you very much.
B. You're welcome.

Clocks:
* 0 - 60
* o'clock
* hour(s)
* minute(s)

Idiom:

● ●
Pick you up.
*I will come and get you.
I will pick you up at 8:00.

A. When can we meet?
B. I can meet you at _____.
A. Okay, I'll pick you up at _____.

January 1, 2013

Days

Sunday
Monday
Tuesday
Wednesday
Thursday
Friday
Saturday

Sunday	Monday	Tuesday	Wednesday	Thursday	Friday	Saturday
					1	2
3	4	5	6	7	8	9
10	11	12	13	14	15	16
17	18	19	20	21	22	23
24	25	26	27	28	29	30

Months

January
February
March
April
May
June
July
August
September
October
November
December

A. Excuse me, what <u>day</u> is this?
B. It's _____.
A. Thank you very much.
B. You're welcome.

A. Excuse me, what is the <u>date</u>?
B. It's _____. (USA- *month, day, year*)
A. Thank you very much.
B. You're welcome.

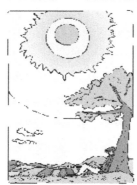

Time Words:
* yesterday
* today
* tomorrow
* morning
* afternoon
* evening
* month, day, year

Questions and Answers:
What did you do <u>yesterday</u>?
Yesterday I ___.
What did he do <u>today</u>?
Today he ___.
What will she do <u>tomorrow</u>?
Tomorrow she will ___.
Where are we going this <u>morning</u>?
This morning we are going ___.
What will they do this <u>afternoon</u>?
This afternoon they will ___.
Where are you going this <u>evening</u>?
This evening I am going to ___.

4 Weather & Animals

The Flood

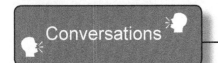
Conversations

Part 1

A. What was the weather like yesterday?
B. It was ___.
A. What is the weather like today?
B. It is _____.
A. What's the forecast for tomorrow?
B. It will be _____.

Weather Forecast

Verb: be
Future tense of *to be*:
I will be___.
He/She will be ___.
You will be ___.
It will be ___.
We will be ___.
They will be ___.

A. <u>Yesterday,</u> I got <u>wet,</u> because it was <u>raining</u>.
B. <u>Today,</u> I am <u>cold,</u> because it is <u>snowing</u>.
C. <u>Tomorrow</u> it will be <u>hot,</u> because the
      temperature will be about 100° F.

because - the reason, why

SEASONS

Summer - Winter - Spring - Fall (Autumn)

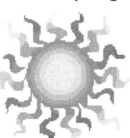

spring
cloudy
raining
rainy
wet

summer
sunny
hot
dry

winter
snowing
snowy
cold

fall / autumn
mild
windy
chilly

Yesterday - Today - Tomorrow

Song: "Old Man Noah Had a Boat"
  tune - Old McDonald
  Old man Noah had a boat.
  e-i-e-i-o
  And on this boat he had a <u>dog</u>.
  e-i-e-i-o
  with a <u>bow-wow</u> here and a <u>bow-wow </u>there
  (make the sound of the animal)
  Here a <u>bow-wow</u> there a<u> bow-wow</u> everywhere a <u>bow-wow.</u>
  Old man Noah had a boat.
  e-i-e-i-o

Pronunciation

s	t	b	short o
seasons	**t**o	**b**e	h**o**t
summer	**t**wo	**b**ut	**O**ctober
spring	**t**oday	**b**ad	**o**n
sister	**t**omorrow	**b**irds	n**o**t
south	**t**ime	**b**ecause	*G**o**d
sunny	**T**uesday	***b**elieved	*d**o**gs
snow		***b**uild	
***s**end		***b**oat	
***s**in			
***s**aved			
***s**ign			

Rhythm

cold
mild
rain
snow
clouds
wind
cats
dogs
*pig
*goat
*sheep
*cow
*horse
*duck

weather
forecast
summer
winter
autumn
***rain**bow
***No**ah
***wor**shiped
***prom**ised
***judge**ment

snowy
snowing
rainy
raining
cloudy
sunny
windy
seasons
***rab**bit
***chick**en
***hors**es
***mon**key
***cam**el
***sin**ful

*Asterisks indicate Part 2 words.

IDIOMS

I smell a rat.
* I think something is wrong.
The man on TV wants me to buy the product, but <u>I smell a rat</u>.

It's for the birds.
* It is not important. It"s not good.
That movie was <u>for the birds</u>.

It's raining cats and dogs.
*There was a lot of rain.
Last night <u>it was raining cats and dogs</u>.

43

Part 1

THE FLOOD

All of the people were very sinful, except Noah and his family.
They worshiped and obeyed God.
God told Noah to build a boat, because He was going to flood the earth.
God told Noah to go into the boat with his family and many animals.

Definitions:

All of the people were very sinful, except Noah and his family.

All - total, everyone
people - humans
were - past tense plural of *be*
         (review INTRO lesson)
sinful - very evil
except - <u>not</u> Noah and his family
Noah - a good man

They worshiped and obeyed God.

worshiped - honored

God told Noah to build a boat, because he was going to flood the earth.

told - past tense of *tell*; to say something
to build - put together
a boat - man-made thing that floats
was going - past continuous of verb
    to be going
to flood - cover with water

God told Noah to go into the boat with his family and many animals.

animals -- any living thing except plants
    and man

Grammar: verbs

	Present		Past
I	worship	I	worshiped
you	worship	you	worshiped
he	worships	he	worshiped
she	worships	she	worshiped
it	worships	it	worshiped
we	worship	we	worshiped
they	worship	they	worshiped

Discussion Questions:

1. What were the people like?
2. Who worshiped God?
3. What did God tell Noah to do? Why?
4. Who went into the boat? Why?

Part 2

Everything died except the people and the animals in the boat.
God saved the animals and Noah's family, because they believed
and obeyed God.
God promised, " I will never flood the whole earth again."
The rainbow is the sign of God's promise.

Taken from Genesis 6,7 & 8

Grammar: verbs

Present		Past	
I	save	I	saved
you	save	you	saved
he	saves	he	saved
she	saves	she	saved
it	saves	it	saved
we	save	we	saved
they	save	they	saved

Present		Past	
I	believe	I	believed
you	believe	you	believed
he	believes	he	believed
she	believes	she	believed
it	believes	it	believed
we	believe	we	believed
they	believe	they	believed

Definitions:
Everything died except the people and the animals in the boat.
Everything - all
died - stop living
people - men & women
in the boat - a barge type boat
God saved the animals and Noah's family, because they believed and obeyed God.
saved - rescued
believed - put faith in
God promised, " I will never flood the whole earth again."
will never flood - will not cover with water
The rainbow is the sign of God's promise.
rainbow - a half circle of colors
sign - an object to inform people

Present		Past	
I	die	I	died
you	die	you	died
he	dies	he	died
she	dies	she	died
it	dies	it	died
we	die	we	died
they	die	they	died

Future	
I	will flood
you	will flood
he	will flood
she	will flood
it	will flood
we	will flood
they	will flood

Discussion Questions:

1. What/Who died?
2. Who did not die? Why?
3. What did God promise?
4. What is the rainbow?

Part 2

a sheep - sheep

a horse - horses

a goat - goats

a cat - cats

a dog - dogs

A. Have you ever seen a _____?
B. Yes, I have seen a _____.
    No, I have never seen a _____.
A. Have you ever lived on a farm?
B. Yes/No.
A. What kind of animals live on a farm ?
B. _____ live on a farms.

a rabbit - rabbits

Grammar: verbs

Present Perfect	
I, you	have seen
he, she, it	has seen
we, they	have seen

a chicken - chickens

a cow - cows

a pig - pigs

a duck - ducks

a giraffe-giraffes

a monkey - monkeys

an elephant - elephants

a zebra-zebras

a lion-lions

a bear-bears

a tiger-tigers

a parrot-parrots

a water buffalo-buffalos

5   Travel

The Promise through Abraham

Conversations

Part 1

octagon

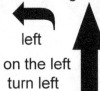

Directions:

straight ahead

left   right

on the left   on the right
turn left   turn right

a map

square

triangle

A. Excuse me, how do I get to the <u>Post Office</u>?
   (Use this map to give directions.
   Start at The Center.)
B. Go <u>west</u> on <u>Main Street</u> one block. It's <u>on the left.</u>

rectangle

circle

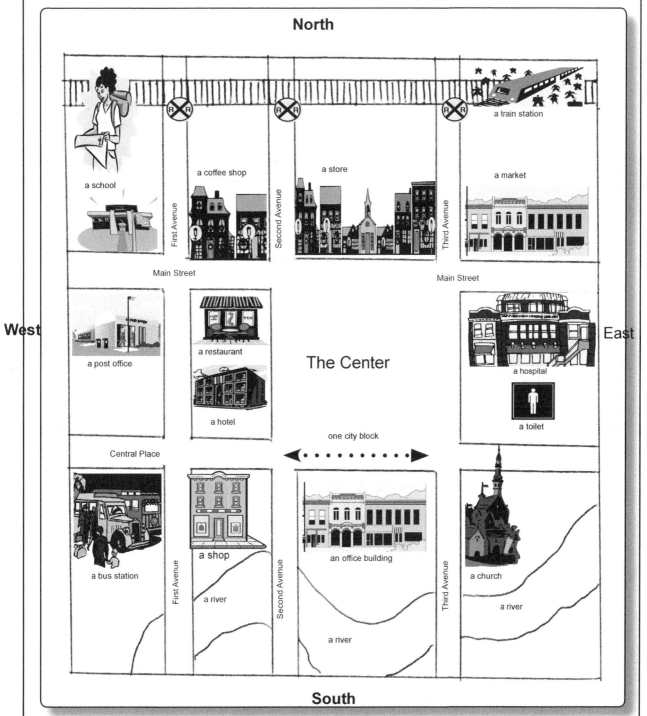

51

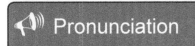
c (s)
center
city
central
offi**c**e
*pla**c**e
*ex**c**ept

r
right
river
restaurant
*rain
*rainy
*raining
*rainbow

st
station
store
star
straight
*ea**st**
*we**st**
*po**st**

long a
str**ai**ght
m**ai**n
r**ai**n
st**a**tion
d**ay**
*n**a**tions
***A**braham
*s**a**ved
*l**a**ter
*w**ai**ted

Rhythm

center
market
office
central
city
river
***af**ter
***man**y
***Sar**ah
***fa**ther
***wait**ed
***la**ter

toilet
building
second
travel
***Jew**ish
***na**tion
***prom**ise
***prom**ised
***chil**dren

avenue
restaurant
bus station
train station
coffee shop
post office
***A**braham
***fam**ily
***fin**ally

* Asterisks indicate Part 2 words.

Personal Map:

Draw on the map below. Put the place you live in the middle. Draw the street on which you live and the connecting streets. Draw some places on the map where you often go.

Examples: schools, stores, parks, etc.

Part 1

The Promise Through Abraham

Many years after Noah, God chose Abraham to be the father of the Jewish nation.
God told him to travel to a new land.
Abraham and his family obeyed.
God promised to bless all nations through him.

<u>Many years after Noah, God chose Abraham to be the father of the Jewish nation.</u>

many - a large number
God chose - past tense of *choose*, to pick
Abraham - the first man in the Jewish and Arab race
Jewish nation- the Israelites

<u>God told him to travel to a new land.</u>

told - past tense of *tell*
to travel - to leave your home
new - opposite of old
land - Israel

<u>Abraham and his family obeyed.</u>

his - possessive pronoun

<u>God promised to bless all nations through him.</u>

promised - past tense of *promise*, to pledge
to bless - to do something good   Review opposites good-bad.
all nations - all people
through him - by Abraham's family, descendents

Grammar: verbs

	Present	Past
I, you	choose	chose
he, she, it	chooses	chose
we, they	choose	chose

Discussion Questions:
1. Who did God choose to be the "Father of the Jews"?
2. What did God tell him to do?
3. What did Abraham and his family do?
4. What did God promise to do?

Part 2

Abraham and his wife, Sarah, waited many years.
They had no children.
Would God keep His promise?
Finally they had a son.
God kept his promise.
Many, many years later God sent the Deliverer through Abraham's family.

Grammar: verbs

 Abraham and his wife waited many years.
waited - past tense of *wait,* to pass time, stay

	Present	Past
I, you	wait	waited
he, she, it	waits	waited
we, they	wait	waited

They had no children.
had - past tense of *have*

	Present	Past
I, you	have	had
he, she, it	has	had
we, they	have	had

Would God keep His promise?
would keep- verb is conditional on God
Finally they had a son.
finally - in the end
God kept his promise.
kept - past tense of *keep*, to honor

	Present	Past
I, you	keep	kept
he, she, it	keeps	kept
we, they	keep	kept

Many, many years later God sent the Deliverer through Abraham's family.
many, many years later - much later,
        42 generations (Matthew 1:17)
sent - past tense of *send*
the Deliverer - Jesus

	Present	Past
I, you	send	sent
he, she, it	sends	sent
we, they	send	sent

MIDDLE EAST

Discussion Questions:
1. Does that include you and me?
2. Did Abraham and Sarah have
    a baby soon?
3. Who did God finally send?
4. Did God keep his promise?
5. Who did God send many, many years later?

Part 2

A. Where is your <u>house</u> on the map?
B. I live at <u>address</u>.
A. Where is the ___ from your home?
B. It is ___.

A. Excuse me. How do I get to ___?
B. Go _____.
A..Thank you very much.

North

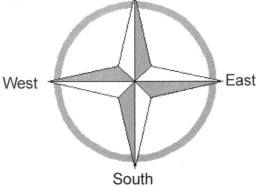

West

East

South

Places:
a school
a store
a mall
a hospital
a train station
a bus station
a hotel
a restaurant
a market
a church
a coffee shop
a post office

Directions:

straight ahead

left

right

on the left
turn left

on the right
turn right

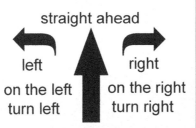

STOP

ONE WAY

YIELD

octagon

square

triangle

R R

circle

DETOUR

rectangle

57

6 Homes

Moses

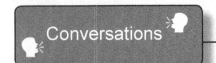
Conversations

Part 1

A. What kind of a home do you have?
B. I live in _____.

a house

a neighbor
a neighborhood

an apartment

a mobile home

A. Where's the ___ ?
B. It's in the ___.

Kitchen

stove

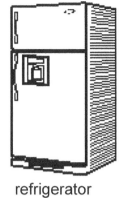

refrigerator

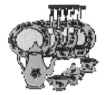

dishes

kitchen cabinets

Living Room

lamp

television

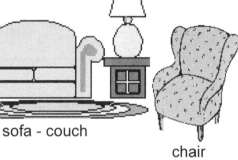

sofa - couch

chair

fireplace

Bedroom

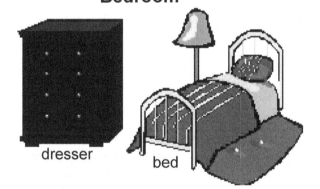

dresser

bed

Bathroom

sink

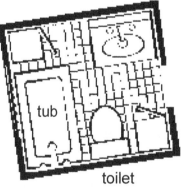

tub

toilet

Dining Room

dining table & chairs

hard g	l	ch	long o
garage	**l**iving	**ch**	s**t**ove
God	**l**amp	**ch**air	h**o**me
get	**l**and	cou**ch**	m**o**bile
getting	**l**eft	**ch**icken	s**o**fa
goat	**l**eave	kit**ch**en	t**o**ld
garden	*l**ead	*****ch**urch	*****o**bey
*****g**reat	*****l**ater	*****ch**ildren	*****ch**ose
*****g**rand			*****M**oses
*****g**rew			

Rhythm 🎵

mobile
sofa
kitchen
dishes
table
*****Mo**ses
*****E**gypt
*****Jew**ish
*****pe**ople

toilet
fireplace
dresser
bathtub
closet
bedroom
*****num**ber
*****some**one
*****ceil**ing
*****pal**ace

cabinets
living room
dining room
mobile home
neighborhood
*****A**braham
*****fam**ily
*****Jew**ish home
*****mov**ing day
*****grand**children
*****pow**erful

* Asterisks indicate Part 2 words.

IDIOMS

Drive someone up a wall
* make someone act crazy
She had a strange laugh that
<u>drove me up the wall.</u>

Directions:

straight ahead

left   right
on the left   on the right
turn left   turn right

Right on!
*You are correct.
He answered the question correctly.
He was <u>right on</u>.

Went through the roof.
* To get very mad
He got so mad that <u>he went through the roof</u>.

Part 1

HOMES

Many years later Abraham's great-grandchildren
  moved to Egypt.
The Jewish family grew in number.
The King of Egypt tried to kill all the baby boys,
  because he was afraid.
He thought the Jews would become powerful.

Many years later Abraham's great-grandchildren moved to Egypt.

Abraham's family - possessive noun, 'This is <u>Mary's dress</u>."
moved - past tense of *move*
to Egypt - a country southwest of Israel
        See the map from the last lesson.

The Jewish family grew in number.

The family - extended family   Many people
              were born over many generations.
grew in number - many in number
        They became at least 2 million people.

**The King of Egypt tried to kill all
the baby boys, because he was afraid.**

tried - past tense of *try*
Moses - famous Jewish leader

**He thought the
Jews would become powerful.**

thought - past tense of *think*
would become - may be
powerful - very strong

Grammar: verbs

	Present	Past
I, you	move	moved
he, she, it	moves	moved
we, they	move	moved

	Present	Past
I, you	grow	grew
he, she, it	grows	grew
we, they	grow	grew

	Present	Past
I, you	try	tried
he, she, it	tries	tried
we, they	try	tried

would - expresses condition

	Present	Past
I, you	become	became
he, she, it	becomes	became
we, they	become	became

	Present	Past
I, you	think	thought
he, she, it	thinks	thought
we, they	think	thought

Discussion:
1. When did this happen?
2. Where did Abraham's family go?
3. What happened to the family?
4 What did the king do? Why?
5. What did the king think?

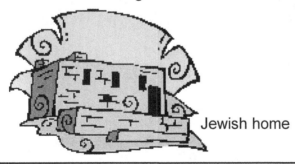

Jewish home

Part 2

God used the king's daughter to save baby Moses.
She found him and raised him in the palace.
He had 2 homes: a Jewish home and the king's palace.
God chose Moses to lead the Jewish people.

 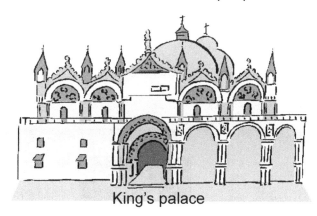

King's palace

God used the king's daughter to save baby Moses.
king's daughter - the princess found Moses in the river.
She found him and raised him in the palace.
palace - a king's home
raised - grew up
He had 2 homes: a Jewish home and the king's palace.
a Jewish home - a poor person's home
God chose Moses to lead the Jewish people.
chose - past tense of *choose;*   I choose Maria, Khai, and Joe.
                                     I <u>chose</u> Maria, Khai, and Joe."

to lead - to go in front

Discussion:
1. Who did God use to save baby Moses?
2. Where did she raise Moses?
3. How many homes did Moses have?
4. Name the homes.
5. Who did God choose to lead the Jews?

Grammar: verbs

	Present	Past
I, you	use	used
he, she, it	uses	used
we, they	use	used

	Present	Past
I, you	find	found
he, she, it	finds	found
we, they	find	found

	Present	Past
I, you	raise	raised
he, she, it	raises	raised
we, they	raise	raised

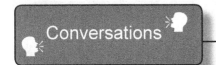

Part 2

It is moving day:

A. Is your apartment on the <u>second</u> floor?
B. Yes.
A. Is there an elevator?
B. No.
A. Then we will have to take (to go up) the stairs.

elevator

stairs

Will you take the <u>elevator</u> or the <u>stairs</u>?

Future	
I	will have
you	will have
he	will have
she	will have
it	will have
we	will have
they	will have

should-expresses necessity and/or obligation
I should ___. ex. I should <u>study English</u>

A. Where should we put the ___?
B. Put the ___ in the ___.

Grammar: verbs

Present		Past	
I	put	I	put
you	put	you	put
he	puts	he	put
she	puts	she	put
it	puts	it	put
we	put	we	put
they	put	they	put

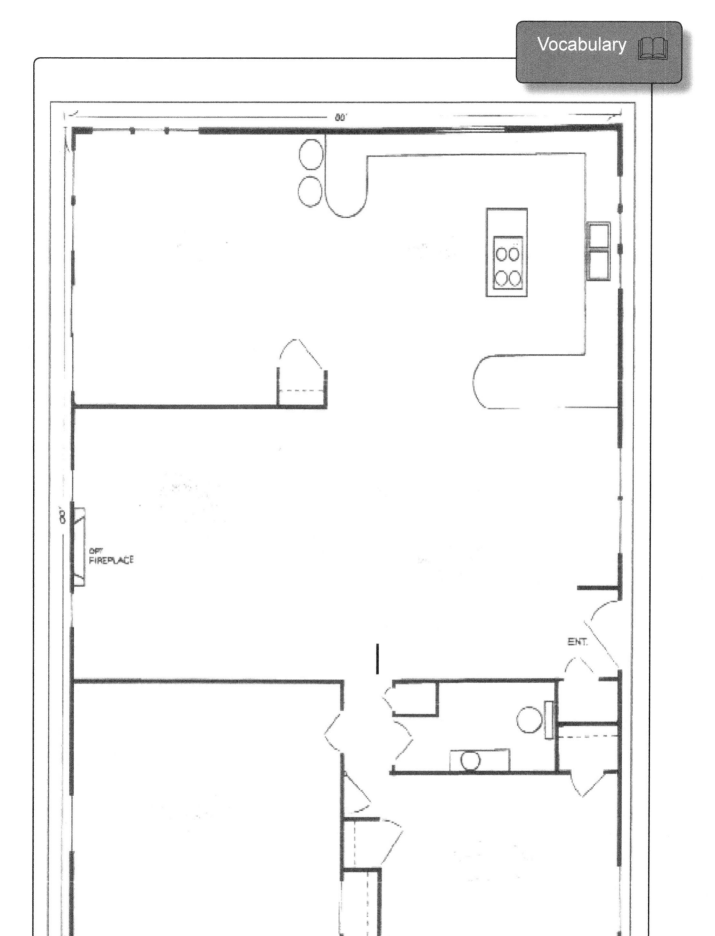

OPT
FIREPLACE

ENT.

7 Food

Passover

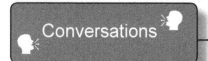
Part 1

What is this? This is a ___.
What is that? That is ____.
What are these? These are _____.
What are those? Those are _____.

Chant
"This. That. These. Those.
Snap your fingers.
Touch your toes".

A. What would you like for <u>breakfast, lunch, dinner</u>?
B. I would like ___. I enjoy eating ___.

Grammar: verbs

Definitions: Modal Auxiliary Verbs

would - expresses condition or desire
    I would (wouldn't) like ___.
    Put many positive or negative choices in the blank.
    example - I would <u>like to go with you</u>.
        I wouldn't <u>do something dangerous.</u>
could - expresses a shade of doubt or a smaller degree of ability
    or possibility
    I could___. example - I could <u>stop the car.</u>
should-expresses necessity and/or obligation
    I should ___. example - I should <u>study English</u>.

	Present	Past
I, you	like	liked
he, she, it	likes	liked
we, they	like	liked

Breakfast

some coffee / tea
some toast
some eggs
some bacon
some cereal
some fruit
some milk
some rice

Lunch

a soda / water
a sandwich
a hamburger
some french fries
some soup
some peanut butter
some jelly

Dinner

meat- chicken, fish, beef
vegetables- corn, cabbage, potatoes, beans
fruit- apples, bananas, grapes, tomatoes
grains- rice, wheat
dairy- milk, yogurt, butter
spices- salt, pepper

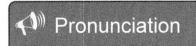

p
peanuts
potato
pepper
palace
put
***p**ower
***P**assover

j
juice
jelly
en**j**oy
***J**ews
***J**ewish

h
hamburger
hot
home
had
***h**ave
***h**ere
***h**orse

long e
t**ea**
coff**ee**
p**ea**nut
b**ee**f
b**ea**ns
wh**ea**t
*r**e**member
*m**ea**l
*n**ee**d
*pl**ea**se

Rhythm

I would like
hamburger
sandwiches
cereal
***Pass**over
***an**ything
***fi**nally

po**ta**to
to**ma**to
ba**nan**a
some **cof**fee
some **ba**con
some **jel**ly
a **sand**wich
*di**rec**tion
*re**mem**ber
*de**liv**er

peanut
butter
bigger
stomach
over
water
***an**gel
***wor**ship
***door**post
***spe**cial
***E**gypt

* Asterisks indicate Part 2 words.

IDIOMS

● Fork it over.
*Give that to me.
Give me all of your money.
<u>Fork it over</u>.

● ● ●
Your eyes are bigger than your stomach.
*You fill your plate with more food that you can possibly eat.
Don't take more food than you can eat. <u>Your eyes are bigger</u>
<u>than your stomach</u>.

73

Part 1

The Jews became slaves.
God said to Moses, "Tell the king to let my people go and worship Me."
The king wouldn't let them leave Egypt.
So God showed His power in many special ways.

Definitions:

The Jews became slaves.

The Jews - the Jewish people, the people descended from Abraham through
          Issac

became - past tense of *become*; example: "I <u>became</u> a teacher."

slaves - one person is owned by another; they work without pay

God said to Moses, "Tell the king to let my people go and worship Me."

tell - present tense

The king wouldn't let them leave Egypt.

wouldn't - would not, a negative choice, See chart- *would, could, should*

let - permit, to give permission; example: *(page 70)*
        "I let ___." Auxiliary verb

leave - go; In this sentence *let leave* go together.

So God showed His power in many special ways.

So - therefore

showed - past tense of *show;*

power - strength; example-electricity

special - unusual, strange, odd

ways - actions, God did things that only God could do
        example - turning water into blood

Grammar: verbs

	Present	Past
I, you	let	let
he, she, it	lets	let
we, they	let	let

	Present	Past
I, you	show	showed
he, she, it	shows	showed
we, they	show	showed

Discussion Questions:
1. What happened to the Jews?
2. What did God tell Moses to tell the king?
3. What wouldn't the king do?
4. What did God do?

Part 2

Finally, God told Moses that He would send the Death Angel.
God told the Jews to kill a lamb and put the blood on the top and sides of the door.
The Death Angel would pass over the houses with the blood on the doorposts.
God would deliver all who obeyed.
This is called the "Passover".
Every year the Jews remember the Passover by eating a special meal.

Definitions:

Finally, God told Moses that He would send the Death Angel.
finally - the end, the last thing;
would send - to tell someone to go and do something
    for you
Death Angel - the angel who was sent
**God told the Jews to kill a lamb and put the blood on the top and sides
of the door.**
lamb - a young sheep
put - place: present and past tense of *put*
blood - red cells in the body that carry life
top and sides- above and left and right
The Death Angel would pass over the houses with the blood on the doorposts.
pass over - go over
doorpost - the frame of the door
God would deliver all who obeyed.
would deliver - would not kill the boys of the houses
    with the blood on the doorposts
This is called the "Passover".
called - past tense of *call*
Passover - the celebration of this time in Jewish history
Every year the Jews remember the Passover by eating a special meal.
Every year - once in 365 days
meal - dinner, feast

Discussion Questions:
1. What did God finally tell Moses?
2. What did God tell the Jews to do?
3. What would the Death Angel do?
4. What is this called?
5 . What do the Jews do every year?
6. Why do you think the Passover meal is important?

Grammar: verbs

	Present	Past
I, you	put	put
he, she, it	puts	put
we, they	put	put

	Present	Past
I, you	pass	passed
he, she, it	passes	passed
we, they	pass	passed

	Present	Past
I, you	deliver	delivered
he, she, it	delivers	delivered
we, they	deliver	delivered

	Present	Past
I, you	call	called
he, she, it	calls	called
we, they	call	called

	Present	Past
I, you	remember	remembered
he, she, it	remembers	remembered
we, they	remember	remembered

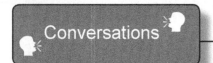
Part 2

A: Are you going to the market/grocery store?
B: Yes, I am. What would you like?
A: I would like _____.

Vocabulary
*Review the vocabulary from Part 1 and practice these words.

| market | grocery | store | aisle |
| where's | are going | how much | costs |

At the market:
A: Excuse me, where's the ___?
B: Yes. It 's on aisle __.

A: Excuse me, how much is the ___?
B: It costs ___.

I Am Going to the Market

Make a circle and the first person starts by saying,
"I am going to the market, and in my cart I put (name a food item)."
The next person says,
"I am going to the market and in my cart I put (name the same item and add a new one)."
Each person says the same sentence plus the items mentioned before and then adds a new one. This is a good memory game and vocabulary practice.

Chant:
A: Where's Charlie?
B: He's in the kitchen.
A: What's he doing?
B: He's eating ___.

Practice

Say the amounts of money below.
Write 5 more of your own and say them to a partner.

$1.05 - one dollar and five cents
$25.74 - twenty-five dollars and seventy-four cents
$114.99 - one-hundred-fourteen dollars and ninety-nine cents

$53.68 - fifty-three dollars and sixty-eight cents
$80.04 - eighty dollars and four cents
$16.33 - sixteen dollars and thirty-three cents

Money

coins
penny - $.01, 1¢
nickel - $.05, 5¢
dime - $.10, 10¢
quarter - $.25, 25¢

paper
one-dollar bill - $1.00
five-dollar bill - $5.00
ten-dollar bill - $10.00
twenty-dollar bill - $20.00

8   Laws

Ten
Commandments

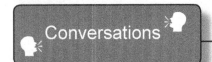
Part 1

laws - rules made by governments
penalty - what happens if you don't obey the laws

triangle

I want to learn to drive.
What should I do?

rectangle

	Present	Past
I, you	want	wanted
he, she, it	wants	wanted
we, they	want	wanted

Driving
*Get a Driving Manual to
  study the driving laws.
* Wear your seatbelt.
*Children should be buckled
  into a safety seat.
*Don't talk on a cellphone.
*Don't drink alcohol and then drive.
*Obey the driving laws.

I just had a wreck in my car.
What should I do?

*Always stop.
*Check to see if anyone is hurt.
*Call 911 to report the accident.

Laws about children:
* Never leave children in the
  car without an adult.
*Never leave children at
  home alone.

These are national symbols of the USA.

National Bird-eagle

United States Capitol
Washington DC

Flag symbols
13 stripes - 13 colonies
50 stars - 50 states
red - blood of soldiers
white - peace
blue - freedom

National Song - Star Spangled Banner

l
laws
local
license
later
*leave
*living
*led
*lie

al (əl)
penalty
manual
national
special
local

bl
blue
blood
black
blond
*blizzard
*block
*blessed

sh
fish
show
showed
should
Washington
*worship

-er
driver
over
banner
never
*later
*Passover
*together
*remember

short a
flag
happens
accident
banner
*capitol
*national
*command

Rhythm ♫

adult
alone
without
report
*before
*away
*command
*obey

penalties
government
vehicle
accident
*anyone
*driving laws
*traffic laws

national
capitol
Washington
colonies
*everything
*manual
*special laws

* Asterisks indicate Part 2 words.

IDIOMS

● ●
Face the music.
* To take responsibility for your actions
He committed a crime and had to
<u>face the music.</u>

●
On ice
* To set aside for later use or safekeeping
Let's keep that idea <u>on ice</u> for awhile.

●
You blew it.
* You have failed at a task or situation.
He started taking drugs. He <u>blew it.</u>

● ●
Bend over backwards
* To go out of your way to help someone
He <u>bent over backwards</u> to help his brother.

Laws   Part 1

Moses led the Jews through the desert to the mountain
        where God first talked to him.
Over a million people followed Moses.
They had trouble living together in peace.
God met Moses on the mountain and gave him special laws or
        commands for the people to obey.

Definitions:

Moses led the Jews through the desert to the mountain where God first talked to him.

led - past tense of *lead;*   To go in front of

desert - a dry, barren place.

mountain - a land mass that is higher than a hill.

talked - past tense of *talk;*

Over a million people followed Moses.

Over a million - more than 1,000,000

followed - past tense of *follow,*
        to go behind someone

They had trouble living together in peace.

trouble - a hard time

peace - no war

God met Moses on the mountain and gave him special laws or commands for the people to obey.

met - past tense of *meet,* to face someone

gave - past tense of *give;*

special - something different, valuable

laws or commands - to direct with authority,
        to order someone to do something

Discussion Questions:

1. Who led the Jews?
2. Where did they go?
3. How many people went with Moses?
4. What did they have trouble doing?
5. What did God give Moses on the mountain?

Grammar: verbs

	Present	Past
I, you	lead	led
he, she, it	leads	led
we, they	lead	led

	Present	Past
I, you	talk	talked
he, she, it	talks	talked
we, they	talk	talked

	Present	Past
I, you	follow	followed
he, she, it	follows	followed
we, they	follow	followed

	Present	Past
I, you	meet	met
he, she, it	meets	met
we, they	meet	met

	Present	Past
I, you	give	gave
he, she, it	gives	gave
we, they	give	gave

Part 2

God wrote the laws on stone tablets.

Some of these laws are:

* Only worship God
* Respect your parents
* Be faithful in marriage
* Do not steal
* Do not lie

These laws help us today.

When people break God's laws, they sin and God will judge them.

Countries use these laws to help rule their people.

Taken from Exodus 20

Definitions:

God wrote the laws on stone tablets.

wrote - past tense of *write,*

stone tablet - flat rocks,

Some of these laws are:

* Only worship God - show love to God.
* Respect your parents - love your parents.
* Be faithful in marriage - love your spouse.
* Do not steal - don't take anything that is not yours.
* Do not lie - always tell the truth.

	Present	Past
I, you	write	wrote
he, she, it	writes	wrote
we, they	write	wrote

These laws still help us today.

still help - continue to help.

When people break God's laws, they sin and God will judge them.

break - present tense, do not obey

Countries use these laws to help rule their people.

rule - take care of; govern

Discussion Questions:
1. On what did He write the laws?
2. What are some of the laws?
3. How do these laws help us today?
4. When people break these laws, what happens?
5. How do countries use these laws?
6. Does your home country have any of these laws?

Part 2

Chant
STOP
DROP
ROLL

SAFETY

At Home

Be careful with fire: candles, fireplaces, stoves, cookers, burning trash
Keep matches away from children.
Always keep a fire extinguisher handy. Put one in the kitchen.
Put in smoke alarms.
Put guns in a locked place.
Teach children to put away toys after playing with them.
Keep medicine in a safe place.
Keep cleaning products away from small children.

At School

Never take medicine from anyone except the school nurse.
Tell an adult if anyone threatens you or anyone else.
Tell an adult if anyone brings a weapon to school.
Follow school rules about safety. (sports, labs, field trips)

<u>How to send medicine to school</u>
*Get the medicine and put it in your child's backpack.
*Write a note to the school nurse describing how to take the medicine.
*Tell your child to give it to their teacher.

EMPLOYEES -MUST- WASH HANDS BEFORE LEAVING THIS ROOM

At Work

Follow all work safety rules.
Use equipment safely.
Use tools correctly.
Wear protective clothing, hard hats, boots, and safety glasses.

DANGER
DO NOT ENTER
AUTHORIZED PERSONNEL
ONLY

9 Clothes

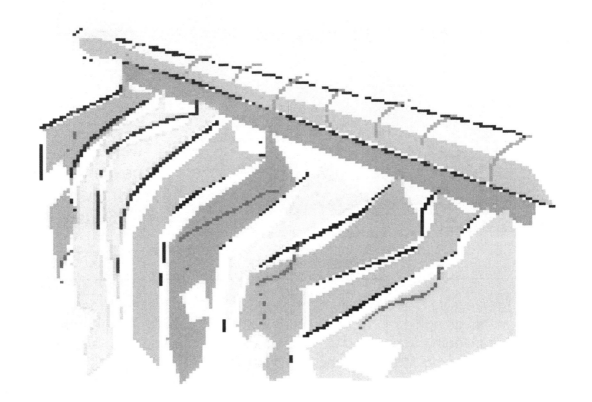

God's
Special Men

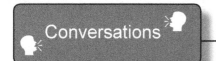
Part 1

Conversations before shopping:

A: Are you going shopping ?
B: Yes. Would you like to come with me?
A. Yes, I would. Where are you going?
B. I am going to <u>the Mall</u>.
(name the store or mall)

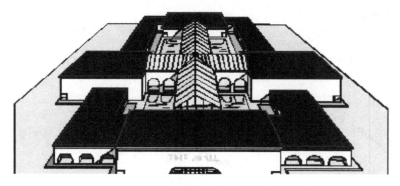

The Mall
The Center
Downtown
The Square

Grammar: verbs

<u>Present Progressive</u>
I   am going
you   are going
he, she, it   is going
we, they   are going

<u>Present Progressive</u>
I   am looking
you   are looking
he, she, it   is looking
we, they   are looking

<u>Present Progressive</u>
I   am having
you   are having
he, she, it   is having
we, they   are having

Conversations while shopping:

A. May I help you?
B. Yes, I am looking for a <u>blue dress</u>.
A. Let me show you what we have.
B. How much does this/these _____ cost?
A. We are having a sale on _____.
     It costs ___.

a shirt
- shirts

a tie
- ties

a suit
- suits

pants

shoes

a dress
- dresses

high heels

Colors

red
pink
purple
yellow
blue
green
brown
black
white

Sizes:
small
medium
large

a hat
- hats

a scarf
- scarves

a shirt & pants

socks

a baseball cap

shoes

shorts

91

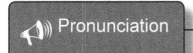
sh
shirt
shoes
shorts
shop
*__sh__opping
*__sh__ow
*__sh__ould

v
scar**v**es
glo**v**es
ele**v**ator
slee**v**e
very
ha**v**ing
*o**v**er
*lea**v**e
*Deli**v**erer

cl
clothes
clothing
climbed
*__cl__ean
*__cl__ock

dr
dress
dresses
dressed
*__dr__ive
*__dr__ink
*__dr__y

pr
pretty
protective
products
proof
*__pr__omised
*__pr__ophets

long i
white
high
tie
tight
descr**i**be
*wh**i**le
*k**i**nd
*B**i**ble
*Mess**i**ah

de**scribe**
dis**cuss**
the **Mall**
the **Square**
high **heels**
a **scarf**
*a **king**

yellow
purple
pretty
handsome
*__god__ly
*__spec__ial
*__col__lar
*__flip__flops
*__proph__ets

secretly
beautiful
medium
*__fol__lowing
*__un__iform

* Asterisks indicate Part 2 words.

IDIOMS

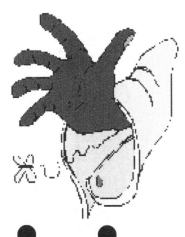

● ●
Up your sleeve
* To plan a secret
What have you got <u>up your sleeve</u>?

● ● ●
Hot under the collar
* Mad, very angry
He was <u>hot under the collar</u>,
because someone stole his car.

● ●
Running a special
* The store is having a sale.
The store is <u>running a special.</u>

● ● ●
Knock someone's socks off
* To really impress someone
He made a good impression.
He <u>knocked our socks off.</u>

● ●
Lose your shirt
* To lose all of your money
   and things
You will <u>lose your shirt</u> if you buy
that car.

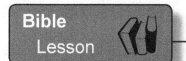
Part 1

God's Special Men

After following Moses for 40 years, the Jews
    entered the Promised Land.
God spoke to the people through godly men
    called prophets.
They wore special clothes to show that they were
    prophets.
When the people did not obey the law,
God warned them through these prophets.
The words of the prophets are in the Bible.
The people wanted a king.

Definitions:

After 40 years the Jews entered the
Promised Land.

entered - past tense of *enter*:
       to come into the country
Promised Land - Israel

God spoke to the people through godly
men called prophets.

spoke - past tense of *speak*: to say words
godly - following God's laws
prophets - men through whom God spoke to the
    people

When the people did not obey the law,
God warned them through these
prophets

warned - past tense of *warn*:
      to tell about danger or punishment to
      come if they didn't obey God's laws
The words of the prophets are in the Bible.

The people wanted a king.

wanted - past tense of *want*: to desire something

Grammar: verbs

	Present	Past
I, you	enter	entered
he, she, it	enters	entered
we, they	enter	entered

	Present	Past
I, you	speak	spoke
he, she, it	speaks	spoke
we, they	speak	spoke

	Present	Past
I, you	warn	warned
he, she, it	warns	warned
we, they	warn	warned

Discussion Questions:
1. How long did it take before the Jews entered the Promised Land?
2. How did God speak to the people?
3. What were they called?
4. What happened when the people didn't obey the law?
5. What did the people want?

Part 2

God chose David to be one of the kings. He also wore special clothes.

God told David and the prophets many things about the Promised Deliverer, the Messiah.

The promises about the Deliverer are written in the Bible.

Many years later the things God told them came true.

	Present	Past
I, you	wear	wore
he, she, it	wears	wore
we, they	wear	wore

Definitions:

God chose David to be one of the kings.

David - the most famous Jewish king

He also wore special clothes.

wore - past tense of *wear:* to put on. David wore royal robes.

God told David and the prophets many things about the Promised Deliverer, the Messiah.

Promised Deliverer - The Deliverer would save the Jews and be their eternal king.

Messiah - the Jewish name for Deliverer

The promises about the Deliverer are written in the Bible.

are- auxiliary verb

written - perfect tense of *write*

Many years later the things God told them came true.

Everything God says is true. Hundreds of prophecies in the Bible have already happened exactly the way God said it would, so it makes sense that the future prophecies in the Bible will come true.

Discussion Questions:
1. Who did God choose to be one of the kings?
2. What did David wear?
3. Who did God tell David and the prophets about?
4. What is the Jewish name for the Deliverer?
5. Where are the promises about the Deliverer written?
6. Are God's promises true? Do you know any of the promises?

Conversations

Part 2

A. What kind of clothes do you need?
B. I need a _____ for_____.

a blouse

a skirt

Grammar: verbs

	Present	Past
I, you	need	needed
he, she, it	needs	needed
we, they	need	needed

A. Is that a new _____? It looks ___ on you.
B. Thanks, I like your ___, too.

Choosing the clothes you will wear each day:
A. What should I wear to _____?
  I think I will wear_____.

flipflops

sneakers

Work Clothes

a suit
- suits

a uniform
- uniforms

a shirt
& pants

ADJECTIVES
pretty
beautiful
handsome
small
medium
large

School Clothes

a t-shirt

a jacket

jeans

athletic shoes

school uniforms

a shirt

a dress

blue jeans

shoes

97

10 Special Days

Jesus' Birth

Part 1

A. When is your birthday?
B. It is _____.
A. What do you do to celebrate your birthday?
B. I _____.

Grammar: verbs

Birthdays:

We have special parties to celebrate birthdays. People invite their friends to the party. We sing "Happy Birthday" and have a special cake. We put candles on the cake. One candle for each year of life. The person who is celebrating their birthday is supposed to make a wish and blow out the candles.
How do you celebrate birthdays in your country?

	Present	Past
I ,you we,they	do have invite	did had invited
he,she it	does has invites	did had invited

A. Are you graduating?
B. Yes.
A. When are you graduating?
B. I am graduating _____.
A. What school are you graduating from?
B. I am graduating from _____.
A. What is your major?
B. My major is _____.

Present Progressive	
I	am graduating
you	are graduating
he, she, it	is graduating
we, they	are graduating

Graduations:

Graduations are a special time of celebration for all of the hard work a person has done to get a college degree. Graduation announcements are sent out to invite people to a graduation ceremony. In the ceremony a diploma is awarded for the specific work that was done. A cap and gown in the school colors is worn in the ceremony. Many people have a party with their friends and family, and presents are given to the one who is graduating.

bouquet

cake - a dessert
candles - things made of wax and string to burn

celebrate, celebrating, celebration - to show joy for something good that has happened
invite - ask people to come and celebrate with you

presents

horns & hats & balloons

a pinata

graduating, graduation - when you finish school
college - a school, university
diploma - the paper showing the degree earned
degree - the finished work for your major
major - the subject you studied
congratulations - a word to tell someone that they did a good job
announcement - a letter or card telling the time and place of the graduation ceremony, and the name of the person graduating

101

bl
blow
blanket
black
blue
*Bi**bl**e
*****bl**ood
*****bl**essed

x (ks)
wa**x**
tu**x**edo
e**x**citing
e**x**change
e**x**cept
*****ex**cuse
*****ex**plain

ow (ou)
v**ow**
d**ow**n
t**ow**n
g**ow**n
br**ow**n

pl
please
planned
cou**pl**es
pledge
peo**pl**e
*pur**pl**e

ch (k)
Christ
Christmas
Christian
*s**ch**ool
*s**ch**olar

short u
up
under
r**u**nning
s**u**pposed
*j**u**st
*Jes**u**s
*yo**u**ng

 Rhythm

celebrate
graduate
*****wed**ding dress
*****hon**eymoon
*****dec**orate
*****Naz**areth
*****Beth**lehem

an**nounce**ment
di**plo**ma
dis**cour**age
*tu**x**edo
*ex**cit**ing

cele**bra**tion
decor**a**tions
gradu**a**tion
happy **birth**day
*Are you **mar**ried?
*love for**ev**er
*a young **wo**man
*special **ba**by

* Asterisks indicate Part 2 words.

IDIOMS

A wet blanket
* A person who discourages people
Don't be <u>a wet blanket</u>.

Kick up your heels
* Do something fun or exciting
Let's go out tonight and <u>kick up our heels.</u>

Party animal
* Someone who likes to have fun a lot.
He's just a <u>party animal</u>.

Different strokes for different folks.
* People do different things because they are all different.

103

Part 1
Jesus' Birth

At just the right time God sent an angel to a young woman named Mary.   He told her that she was going to have a special baby. This baby was God in a human body. The angel said to name him "Jesus the Savior," because he would save his people from their sins.

Definitions:
At just the right time God sent an angel to a young woman named Mary.

just the right time - at the correct time in history

angel - a spirit messenger sent from God

He told her that she was going to have a special baby.

teenage - 13,14,15,16,17,18,19 years old

was going - past progressive

This baby was God in a human body.

human - a person

body - the form

The angel said to name him "Jesus the Savior," because he would save his people from their sins.

said - past tense of *say;* to talk to someone

Jesus - the Son of God

Savior - someone who saves

sins - thoughts and actions that are against God's teaching

Grammar: verbs

	Past Progressive
you we they	were going were born
I he she it	was going was born

	Present	Past
I you we they	send tell say grow	sent told said grew
he she it	sends tells says grows	sent told said grew

Discussion Questions:
1. When did God send the angel to Mary?
2. What was the message to Mary"
3. What was this baby?
4. What was his name?
5. What does Savior mean?
6. What is sin?

Part 2

He was the Promised Deliverer.
He was born in Bethlehem.
God told the shepherds about his birth, and they went to see him.
Jesus grew up in Nazareth.
Today we celebrate Jesus' birth on Christmas Day.

Definitions:
He was the Promised Deliverer.
Promised Deliverer - Jesus
He was born in Bethlehem.
born - come to life
Bethlehem - a town 5 miles south of Jerusalem
See Bethlehem on the map.
God told the shepherds about his birth,
and they went to see him.
shepherd - a person who takes care of sheep
birth - to be born
See pictures of shepherds
Jesus grew up in Nazareth.
grew up - to grow in body and mind
Nazareth - A town 50 miles north of Jerusalem
See Nazareth on the map.
Today we celebrate Jesus' birth on Christmas Day.
Christmas Day - December 25

Discussion Questions:
1. Who was the Promised Deliverer?
2. Where was he born?
3. Who did God tell about his birth?
4. What did they do?
5. Where did Jesus grow up?
6. When do we celebrate Jesus' birth?

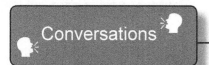
Part 2

> A. Are you married?
> B. Yes/No.
> A. What do you do at a wedding?
> B. We _____.

Weddings: (American)
The wedding usually takes place in a church.
The bride wears a white wedding dress & veil.
The groom wears a tuxedo.
The bride and groom promise to love each other forever.
They are now husband and wife.
After the wedding there is a big party.
The bride and groom cut the wedding cake and receive gifts.
The newly married couple then go on a honeymoon.
What is a wedding like in your country?

> A. Are you married?
> B. Yes/No
> A. When is your anniversary?
> B. It's _____.

Grammar: verbs

	Present	Past
I	take	took
you	wear	wore
we	cut	cut
they	marry	married
he	takes	took
she	wears	wore
it	cuts	cut
	marries	married

Anniversaries:
Each year, on the date of their wedding,
married couples celebrate their wedding anniversary.
Sometimes friends and family have a special party for
the couple.

honeymoon-The married couple go on a trip to celebrate their wedding.

wedding cake- The wedding cake is cut after the wedding and the bride and groom feed a bite to each other.

groom
husband

bride
wife

tuxedo-the groom's suit
wedding dress & veil- the bride's dress and a thin, see-through material worn on the bride's head.

wedding rings-Rings are exchanged during the wedding ceremony as pledges of their love. They are worn on the left hand.

107

11

Jobs

Jesus' Life

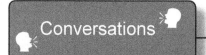
Part 1

A. What do you do?
   (What is your job?)
B. I am a _____.
A. What are your duties?
B. I _____.

I am a homemaker.
I take care of my family.

More questions:
   How many hours do you work?
   What kind of training did you have for your job?
   What do you like/dislike about your job?
   How did you get your job?
   Do you want to continue doing this type of work?
      Why or why not?
   How will learning to speak better English help you
      in your job?

I am an office worker.
I work on a computer.

I am a factory worker. We make ___.

I am a nurse. I take care of sick people.

I am a farmer. I grow___.

I am a student.
I am studying <u>English</u> at ____
(name the school).

I am a laborer.
I work on ____.

I am a housekeeper.
I clean houses/ offices.

I am a fisherman. I catch _____.

I am a seamstress.
I make clothes.

I am a waitress.

I am a chef.

We are working in a
restaurant.

111

y
you
your
you're
yes
*yesterday
*yellow
*year

-y
family
duty
factory
study
body
*anniversary
*honeymoon
*marry
*happy

ing
studying
working
helping
growing
*making
*caring
*fishing
*cleaning

soft g
angel
teenage
pledge
marriage
*courage
*discourage
*manage

-s (z)
duties
houses
offices
clothes
*families
*factories

long u
uniforms
beautiful
computer
human
*usual
*usually
*unique

 Rhythm

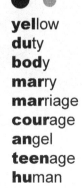

● ○
yellow
duty
body
marry
marriage
courage
angel
teenage
human

○ ● ○
discourage
computer
continue
a student
a farmer
a waitress

● ○ ○
yesterday
factory
honeymoon
studying
offices
factories
uniforms
beautiful
usual

Asterisks indicate Part 2 words.

IDIOMS

● ●
Ax to grind
* complaining, revenge
He had an <u>ax to grind</u>.

● ● ● ●
Don't <u>burn the candle at both ends</u>.
* Don't try to do too many things.
  Don't work all of the time.
She was <u>burning the candle at both ends</u>
at work.

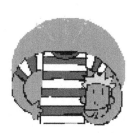

● ●
Stick out your neck
* To go out of your way to
help someone
You <u>stuck out your neck</u>
for me, and I am thankful.

● ●
Don't blow it!
* Don't do something stupid
You have a good relationship with your
girlfriend. <u>Don't blow it</u>!

Song - "Jesus Loves Me"

Jesus loves me this I know,
For the Bible tells me so.
Little Ones to Him belong,
They are weak, but He is strong.
Yes, Jesus loves me (repeat 3 times)
The Bible tells me so.

Bible
Lesson

Part 1

Jesus' Life

Jesus helped Joseph in his carpenter shop.   He studied God's Word every day.   He never sinned, because He was God. When Jesus was thirty, He began to teach God's Word. He did many miracles to show His power and love.

Definitions::

Jesus helped Joseph in his carpenter shop.
helped - past tense of *help*
Joseph - Mary's husband, Jesus' stepfather
carpenter - a person who builds things out of wood
shop - a place to work
He studied God's Word every day.
studied - past tense of *study*
God's Word - the Bible
He never sinned, because He was God.
never - no, not
sinned - past tense of *sin*
When Jesus was thirty, he began to teach God's Word.
began - past tense of *begin*
teach - tell people things that they want to learn
He did many miracles to show His power and love.
did - past tense of *do*
miracles - something only God can do

Discussion Questions:
1. What did Jesus do as he grew up?
2. Who did he help?
3. What did he study?
4. How often did he study?
5. How old was Jesus when he began to teach God's Word?
6. What is a miracle?
7. Why did he do miracles?

Grammar: verbs

	Present	Past
I you we they	help study begin do	helped studied began did
he she it	helps studies begins does	helped studied began did

Part 2

He healed sick people, controlled the weather, and even brought dead people back to life. One time He fed thousands of people with a little boy's lunch.   Many people believed Jesus was the Deliverer.
　　Some loved Him.
　　Others hated Him.

Definitions:

He healed sick people,
healed - past tense of *heal*
sick - ill
controlled the weather.
controlled - past tense of *control*; command
weather - the condition of the air
and even brought dead people back to life.
brought - past tense of *bring*; to lead, to call
dead - not alive
back to life - alive
One time He fed thousands of people with a little boy's lunch.
fed - past tense of *feed*; to eat food
Many people believed Jesus was the Deliverer.
Deliverer - the person promised since the beginning
Some loved Jesus.
loved - past tense of *love*; to care a lot about someone
Others hated him.
Others - different people
hated - past tense of *hate*;
　　to have a strong dislike for someone

Discussion Questions:
1. Do you believe in miracles?
2. What kind of miracles did Jesus do?
3. What did people think about Jesus?
4. Why did some people love Jesus?
5. Why do you think some people hated Jesus?
6. How do YOU feel about Jesus?

Grammar: verbs

	Present	Past
I	heal	healed
you	control	controlled
we	bring	brought
they	feed	fed
	love	loved
	hate	hated
he	heals	healed
she	controls	controlled
it	brings	brought
	feeds	fed
	loves	loved
	hates	hated

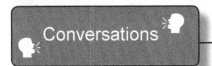
Conversations

Part 2

> A. I am having trouble at work.
> B. What is the problem?
> A. (Tell the problem.)

How to be successful at work:
Always be polite.
Always do your best work.
Get to work on time.
Don't get into arguments with people at work.
Talk to your boss if you are having trouble with someone.
Correct mistakes as quickly as possible.
Make it clear that your family comes first.

> A. How do I become a citizen?
> B. You have to apply to become a citizen.
> A. How do I apply?

How to become a citizen of USA.
1. Submit an application and fee. Check to see what the current fees are.
    (www.uscitzenship.info)
2. You will receive a letter to let you know that your application has been
    accepted. It will tell you where to go to get your fingerprints taken.
3. Then you will be scheduled for an interview and test. They are in
    English.
4. When you pass the interview and test, you will be notified when to come
    to the swearing in ceremony nearest your home.
5. At the ceremony you will become a citizen of the USA.
    (See www.immigrationdirect.com for more information)

Definitions:

trouble - something is not right, not good, a problem

success, sucessful - to be happy with your work

polite - good actions and words

argument - talking to someone in a bad way about an idea that you have
    that is different than their idea

correct - to make something right

mistakes - things that you do wrong that you don't mean to do

possible - as you can

Definitions:

citizen - a person who lives legally in a country

apply, application - put information on a paper to get something

submit - give the paper to the correct people

fee - money paid for a purpose

will receive - future tense of receive; to get something

fingerprints - to put ink on your fingers and press them to a paper

scheduled - to give a time to meet

interview - one person asks another person questions

test - written and / or oral questions to see if a person has learned
    something

notified - to tell someone something by letter or email

swearing in ceremony - promise to obey the laws

12

Communication & Education

Jesus' Message

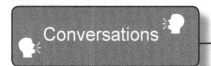
Part 1

A. I am having trouble telling how I feel.
   How do I tell people what I am feeling?
B. Let's talk about feelings.
A. I feel ____.
   When I feel ____, I ____.

A. I think I need more training/education.
B. What would you like to learn?
A. I would like to learn <u>to speak English</u>.
B. Why do you want to learn <u>English</u>?
A. I want to learn <u>English</u> because ____.

<u>Things to learn</u>
automotive repair
to be an electrician
to be a plumber
construction work
welding
truck driving
to be a beautician
nursing
cooking
computer skills
taxi driver

Feelings

energetic - tired

happy - sad

cheerful - grouchy

joyful - depressed

brave - afraid

excited - bored

peaceful - nervous

proud - ashamed

tr
try
training
trouble
truth
wai**tr**ess
trash
trees
triangle

br
brave
brother
bride
brown
bring
brought
A**br**aham

v
valuable
uni**v**ersity
dri**v**ing
gi**v**ing
automoti**v**e
ner**v**ous
*whoe**v**er
*pro**v**ided
*di**v**ided

gr
grouchy
hun**gr**y
an**gr**y
groom
graduating
growing
green
gray

ly
honest**ly**
clear**ly**
quick**ly**
fami**ly**
usual**ly**
safe**ly**
correct**ly**

or
sh**or**t
m**or**e
st**or**y
f**or**
sophom**or**e
bef**or**e

Rhythm

arguing
differences
happening
*****pun**ishment
*****far**away
*****ev**eryone
*****cel**ebrate

● ○ ○

ex**cit**ed
con**struc**tion
beau**tic**ian
an**oth**er
com**pu**ter
*to**geth**er
*e**ter**nal
*pro**vid**ed
*com**pas**sions

○ ● ○

auto**mo**tive
edu**ca**tion
elec**tric**ian
*ener**get**ic
*resur**rec**tion

○ ○ ● ○

* Asterisks indicate Part 2 words.

IDIOMS

Bury the hatchet
* Quit arguing and work out any differences that you may have with another person
Mary and I have been arguing for a year. It is time to <u>bury the hatchet.</u>

If the shoe fits, wear it.
* If something is said that describes you, then it is meant for you
I need to accept the fact that I am shy. <u>If the shoe fits, wear it.</u>

Smell a rat
* Something bad is happening
The salesman is giving me a good deal, but <u>I smell a rat.</u>

Feed someone a line
* To lie
The car salesman is telling me how low the mileage is on this car, but I think he is <u>feeding me a line.</u>

Sell someone short
* To think a person or thing is less valuable
I think you are <u>selling him short</u>. He has been a great help.

Part 1

Jesus' Message

When Adam and Eve sinned God promised to send a Deliverer.
God loved people so much that he came to earth himself as a man.
Jesus came to take the punishment for all the sins of mankind.
By living a perfect life, without any sin, Jesus provided a way to bring people and God together again.
The payment was Jesus' death, and the resurrection was the proof.
God so loved the world that He gave His only Son that whoever believes in
      Him will not die, but have eternal life.
Jesus is the Promised Deliverer.

Taken from the book of John

Discussion Questions:
1. When did God promise the Deliverer?
2. What did God do because He loved people?
3. What did Jesus come to do?
4. Did He live a perfect life without sin?
5. What did Jesus provide?
6. What is the payment for sin?
7. Did Jesus pay for our sin or His sin?
8. What was the proof that He paid for our sin?
9. Whoever believes in Jesus will have what?
10. What does it mean to *believe in Him?*
11. Who delivers us from death?
12. Who is Jesus?

When Adam and Eve sinned God promised to send a Deliverer.

sinned - past tense of *sin*

to send - infinative, to tell someone to go somewhere

God loved people so much that he came to earth himself as a man.

loved - past tense of *love*; to care deeply for someone

himself - reflective pronoun

Jesus came to take the punishment for all the sins of mankind.

punishment - to pay for something someone does that is wrong

all the sins - every bad thing that every person has ever done

mankind - people

By living a perfect life, without any sin, Jesus provided a way

to bring people and God together again.

perfect - without any mistakes or wrongs

provided - past tense of *provide*; to give someone something

to bring - an infinitive meaning to put

together - to combine

again - once more

The payment was Jesus' death, and the resurrection was the proof.

payment - to give something of value

resurrection - to come back to life

proof - to show to be true

God so loved the world that He gave His only son (Jesus),

that whoever believes in him will not die, but have eternal life.

whoever - any person

believes - put faith in, trust

eternal life - to live forever

Grammar: verbs

	Present	Past
I you we they	sin promise love come provide	sinned promised loved came provided
he she it	believes	believed

125

Part 2

Jesus' Stories

Jesus' stories were about common things that the people did, but they were meant to have a lesson in them that would teach people how to live. This was a story Jesus told to teach us that everyone is our neighbor and to treat everyone with kindness. This story has been modernized for us to teach the same message that Jesus taught.

Who Is My Neighbor?

A man was going on the road from ___ to ___. (name 2 local towns)

Suddenly, robbers attacked him. One robber said, "Give me your money." The robbers grabbed everything he had. They beat him up and ran away.

The robbers left the man half dead.

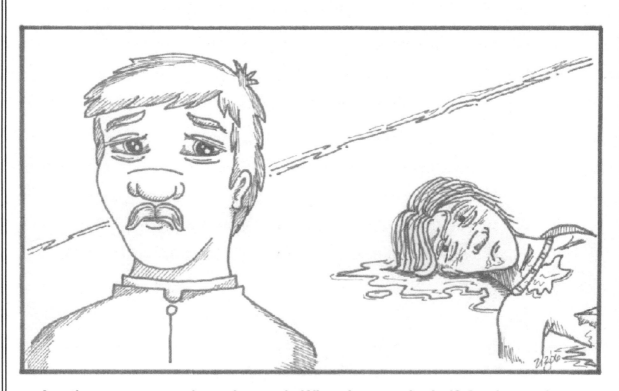

Another man came along the road. When he saw the half dead man, he said, "I don't care. This is none of my business." He walked by on the other side of the road.

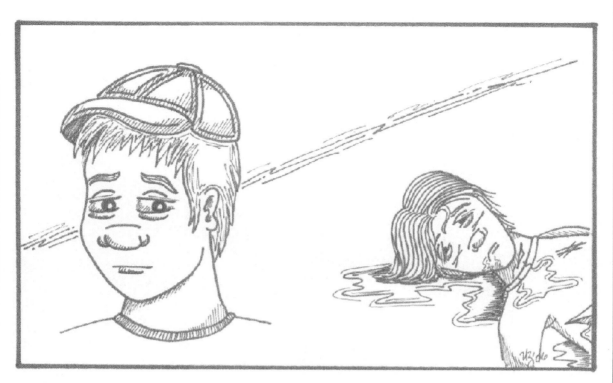

Then a boy came along the road. When he saw the man who was beaten up, he walked by on the other side of the road, too. As he went by him, he laughed and said, "What's your problem? Are you drunk or something?   Oh, it doesn't matter; I don't care about you anyway."

Later another man came along the road. When he saw the man who was beaten up, he felt sorry for him. "I'm sorry. Let me help you."

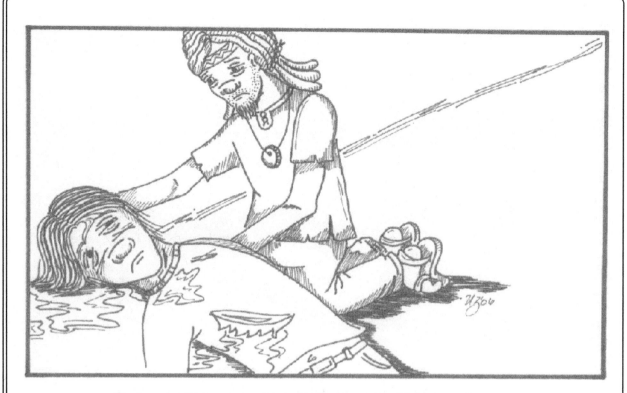

He treated his wounds and took care of him.

Then he took the man to the hospital, where the doctor took care of him.

He gave the doctor some money and said, "Please take care of this man. If you need more money, I will pay you more when I return."

Which one of these three people was a real neighbor to the man who was beaten up by robbers? The one who showed pity.

13

Problems
Health

Jesus' Suffering and Death

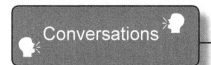 **Conversations**

Part 1

Health Problems

At home:

A. What's the matter?

B. My _____ hurts. (stomach, head, etc)

A. Let's take your temperature. We'll try medicine.
    If it isn't better in a few days we will go to the doctor.

At the doctor:

Patient: I am here to see Dr. Smith.

Receptionist: Please fill out these papers, and give them to me when
        you are finished.(Take someone with you who can tell the
        doctor about illnesses and immunization shots.)

Nurse: (Calls your name.) How are you today?

Patient: Not so good.

Nurse: Where is the pain?

Patient: It's here (point to the place that hurts).

Nurse: The doctor will be in to see you soon.

Doctor: How are you doing?

Patient: Not very good/well. My ___ hurts.

Doctor: Let's have a look at you.
        Take a deep breath. Again.
         Does it hurt when I press here?

Patient: Yes. (No).

Doctor: Let's take your temperature and blood pressure.
         I think you have <u>an infection</u>.
         Here is a prescription for some medicine.

Patient: Thank you doctor.

Doctor: Your welcome. Good-bye.

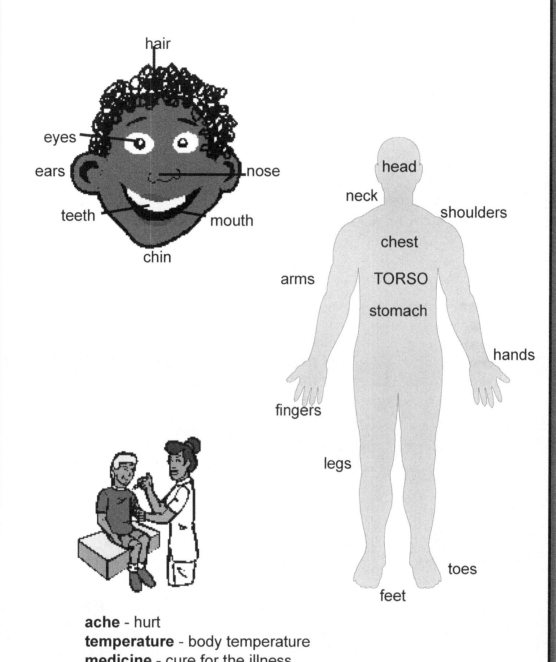

ache - hurt
temperature - body temperature
medicine - cure for the illness
doctor - person trained to heal
nurse - doctor's helper
blood pressure - how the blood circulates through the body
infection - illness
prescription - medicine recommended by the doctor

-tion
prescrip**tion**
infec**tion**
immuniza**tion**
conversa**tion**
applica**tion**
communica**tion**

-th
heal**th**
brea**th**
tee**th**
mou**th**
dea**th**
wi**th**
tru**th**

k
kill
kind
ta**k**ing
li**k**e
too**k**
as**k**
earthqua**k**e

ear
t**ear**
h**ear**
n**ear**
y**ear**
f**ear**

short a
b**a**ck
h**a**ve
st**a**nd
f**a**cts
m**a**d
m**a**tter
asked

short e
h**e**alth
probl**e**ms
pr**e**ss
w**e**ll
h**e**ad
n**e**ck
l**e**gs
ch**e**st
evidence

Rhythm

● ○
shoulders
pressure
patient
problems
matter
stomach
torso
fingers

● ○ ○
medicine
illnesses
suffering
*****wood**en cross
*****pun**ishment
*****Pass**over
*****sac**rificed

○ ● ○
in**fec**tion
pre**scrip**tion
to **stand** on
*to **kill** him
*the **bod**y
*of **Je**sus
*for**give** them

* Asterisks indicate Part 2 words.

IDIOMS

● ●

Get on my nerves
* Makes me mad
She talks too much.
She <u>gets on my nerves</u>.

● ●

Get off my back
* Leave me alone
Okay, I made a mistake. So <u>get off my back</u>.

● ● ●

Doesn't have a leg to stand on
* Doesn't have any support or truth
He doesn't know the facts.
He <u>doesn't have a leg to stand on.</u>

● ●

sick and tired
* I don't like it.
<u>*I'm sick and tired*</u> of working hard.

137

Part 1
Jesus' Suffering and Death

The Jewish priests hated Jesus and wanted to kill him, but only the Roman ruler
could sentence someone to death.
So the Jewish leaders lied about Jesus in a trial, and he was sentenced to die.
Soldiers nailed His hands and feet to a wooden cross.
Even as he was dying on the cross, he asked God to forgive them.
At 3:00, the time for the Passover lamb to be sacrificed, Jesus said,
"It is finished!"

John 18-19

The Jewish priests hated Jesus and wanted to kill him,
priests - religious leaders
hated - past tense of *hate*; to dislike a great deal
wanted - past tense of *want*; to wish for something
to kill - to cause someone to die

but only the Roman ruler could sentence someone to death.
only - There was just one Roman ruler.
Roman ruler - the governor of that place
sentence - legal term meaning the punishment for a crime

So the Jewish leaders lied about Jesus in a trial, and he was sentenced to die.
lied - past tense of *lie*; to tell something false
trial - a court with witnesses

Soldiers nailed His hands and feet to a wooden cross.
nailed - past tense of *nail*

Even as he was dying on the cross, he asked God to forgive them.
Even as - just as
cross - wooden posts on which the criminal is nailed to die
forgive - to pardon someone

At 3:00, the time for the Passover lamb to be sacrificed,
Jesus said, "It is finished!"
the Passover lamb was killed at 3:00 in the afternoon
Passover lamb - a lamb was killed to cover the sins of the person
sacrificed - past tense of *sacrifice;* to give up something of value for the sake of

Discussion Questions:
1. Who hated Jesus?
2. What did they want to do to Jesus?
3. Who could sentence someone to death?
4. What did they do at the trial?
5. What happened next?
6. What did the soldiers do to Jesus?
7. What did Jesus ask God as he was dying?
7. When did Jesus die?
8. What did Jesus say?

Part 2

He was taking the punishment for sin just like the Passover lamb.
Jesus died and there was a great earthquake.
Two rich men who loved Jesus took his body and buried it in a tomb.
The Jewish leaders asked Pilate to put a guard at the tomb and seal it so no
      one would steal the body.
The Jewish leaders thought that was the end of Jesus.

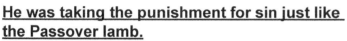

**He was taking the punishment for sin just like
the Passover lamb.**
See Part 1
sin - anything that does not honor God
Jesus died and there was a great earthquake.
died - past tense of *die*
great - big
earthquake - a natural disaster when the ground shakes
Two rich men who loved Jesus took his body and buried it in a tomb.
rich - had a lot of money & things
took - past tense of *take;* to carry
buried - past tense of *bury;* to wrap in cloth and put in a special cave
tomb - burial place
**The Jewish leaders ask Pilate to put a guard at the tomb and seal it so no one
would steal the body.**
Pilate - the Roman ruler of the region
to put a guard - to assign soldiers
seal - proof that the stone was not moved
steal - take away
body - Jesus' body
**The Jewish leaders thought that was
the end of Jesus.**
leaders - Jewish priests
thought - past tense of *think;* to use your brain
end - the finish

Discussion Questions:
1. Why was Jesus being sacrificed?
2. What happened at the moment Jesus died?
3. Who buried Jesus?
4. Where did they bury Jesus' body?
5. What did the Jewish leader ask of Pilate?
6. What did the Jewish leader think?

Grammar: verbs

	Present	Past
I you we they	lie sentence nail ask sacrifice finish	lied sentenced nailed asked sacrificed finished
he she it	lies sentences nails asks sacrifices finishes	lied sentenced nailed asked sacrificed finished

139

Part 2

A: What should you do if ___?
B: I should ___.

Should
* someone loved you
* someone hurt you
* someone helped you
* someone saved your life
* someone asked you for money
* someone hated you
* someone lied about you

Would
* you got lost
* you found something
* you were afraid
* you didn't have a job
* you had no money
* you had no food
* you didn't have a home
* you disobeyed the rules/laws
* you owed someone a lot of money

A: What would you do if ___?
B: I would ___.

Write sentences using these verbs and pronouns.

Sing the Exercise Song-
"Head, Shoulders, Knees, and Toes
   Sing the song as you act out the motions.
      *Head, shoulders, knees and toes
               knees and toes
      Head, shoulders, knees and toes
               knees and toes
   Eyes and Ears and mouth and nose
   Head, shoulders, knees and toes
               knees and toes

   *Substitute other body parts in the song.
         example: head, stomach, arm, leg

Grammar: verbs

Regular verbs:

	Present	Past
I you we they	love help save ask hate lie disobey owe	loved helped saved asked hated lied disobeyed owed
he she it	loves helps saves asks hates lies disobeys owes	loved helped saved asked hated lied disobeyed owed

Irregular verbs:

	Present	Past
I you we they	hurt get find don't do have come	hurt got found didn't did had came
he she it	hurts gets finds doesn't does has comes	hurt got found didn't did had came

14

Holidays

Jesus' Resurrection

Conversations

Part 1

A. What holidays do you celebrate?
B. We celebrate _____.
A. When do you celebrate ___?
B. We celebrate ___ on _____.
A. How do you celebrate_____?
B. We _____.

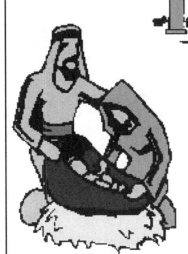

HOLIDAYS:

New Year's Day
  Most countries - January 1
  Chinese - February
  Jewish - September
  Muslim - Dec.-Jan.
Valentine's Day - February 14
Easter - March-April
Passover - March -April
Memorial Day - May
Independence Day
    America - July 4
Thanksgiving - 3rd Thursday of November
Christmas - December 25

New Year's Day

   In most of the world New Year's Day is celebrated on January 1st.
In many Asian countries it is celebrated between January and February.
In some countries New Year comes in March or April. In most countries people celebrate by having parties and counting down the minutes until midnight. Many people shoot fireworks and some give presents.

Valentine's Day

   On Valentine's Day people give the one's they love cards and presents.

Easter - Passover

   Easter is celebrated by Christians as the day Jesus rose from the dead. Also, as a sign of new life, people dye Easter eggs different colors and hide them in the grass for children to find. A family feast is eaten.
Passover is the Jewish celebration of the night the Death Angel passed over their homes in Egypt and their first born sons did not die. A special meal is prepared by Jews.

Memorial Day

   Memorial Day is a day to remember the ones in your family who have died. Many people decorate their family graves with flowers.

Independence Day

   Most countries have a day on which they celebrate their countries' independence. In the USA it is on July 4th.

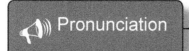
ed (ed)
celebrat**ed**
want**ed**
hat**ed**
trust**ed**
wast**ed**
divid**ed**
recommend**ed**

ed (-d)
li**ed**
di**ed**
lov**ed**
prepar**ed**
*show**ed**
*believ**ed**
*buri**ed**
*roll**ed**

ed (t)
help**ed**
thank**ed**
pass**ed**
ask**ed**
*sacrific**ed**
*finish**ed**
*talk**ed**
*promis**ed**

in
into
inform
information
independence
infection

dis
dishonor
disaster
disobey
dislike
discourage
discuss
***dis**appeared

un
until
unusual
under
understand
unhappy
***un**leaven
***un**divided

 Rhythm

celebrate
holiday
Valentine's
Passover
***rolled** away
***ran** away
***fes**tival
***orn**aments

mem**or**ial
A**mer**ica
un**us**ual
*ex**per**ienced
*He **ate**
  with them.
*He **talked**
  with them.
*De**liv**erer

cele**bra**tion
having **par**ties
until **mid**night
*It was **emp**ty.
*resur**rec**tion
*special
  Christmas

* Asterisks indicate Part 2 words.

IDIOMS

● ● ●

Feel like a million dollars
    * to feel very good
We had a great time at the New Year party. I <u>feel like a million dollars.</u>

●

In stitches
* To laugh for a long time
He had us all <u>in stitches</u>.

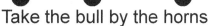

● ● ●

Take the bull by the horns
  * Take charge of your life, take control
He is <u>taking the bull by the horns</u> and not drinking too much anymore.

● ● ●

Give it your best shot
* Do your best work
I don't have much money to spend on the party, but I will <u>give it my best shot.</u>

● ●

Stick to your guns
  * Don't change your mind, continue
     doing what you are doing
They want to change to place for the party.
<u>Stick to your guns</u> and don't let them change.

Part 1

Jesus' Resurrection

   Three days later some women came to the tomb. They saw that the stone in front of the tomb was rolled away.   They also saw two angels in bright clothes who said, "Jesus is not here. He is alive!"

   The women ran away to tell Jesus' friends. Peter and John ran to the tomb to see if it was true.   The tomb was empty. Was Jesus really alive?

<u>Three days later some women came to the tomb.</u>

tomb - a place to bury dead people

<u>They saw that the stone in front of the tomb was rolled away.</u>

stone - large round rock

rolled - past tense of *roll*; push the stone away

<u>They also saw two angels in bright clothes who said, "Jesus is not here.</u>
<u>He is alive!"</u>

bright - shiny

<u>The women ran away to tell Jesus' friends.</u>

ran - past tense of *run*; to move your legs as fast as you can

<u>Peter and John ran to the tomb to see if it was true.</u>

Peter and John - 2 men who were close friends of Jesus

<u>It was empty.</u>

empty - nothing there

<u>Was Jesus really alive?</u>

really - truly

Discussion:
1. How many days had passed since Jesus died?
2. Who came to the tomb first?
3. What did they see when they got there?
4. What did the angels say?
5. What did the women do next?
6. What did Peter and John do?
7. What did Peter and John find?
8. How do we know this really happened?

Grammar: verbs

	Present	Past
I	roll	rolled
you	run	ran
we	eat	ate
they	rise	rose
	disappear	disappeared
he	rolls	rolled
she	runs	ran
it	eats	ate
	rises	rose
	disappears	disappeared

Part 2

Jesus' Resurrection

That evening Jesus came to the house where the disciples and friends were meeting. He showed them the nail scars in His hands and feet, and he even ate and talked with them.

For 40 days Jesus was seen by many people. They believed He really was the Promised Deliverer.

Then one day, as the disciples were with Jesus, he rose into the air and disappeared into heaven. Two angels came and told the men that Jesus would come back to earth again someday.

That evening Jesus came to the house where the disciples and friends were meeting.

evening - night time

disciples - men and women who followed Jesus and helped him

were meeting - past continuous

He showed them the nail scars in His hands and feet, and he even ate and talked with them.

scars - wounds, places on the skin where you have had an injury

nails - metal pieces used to hold wood together

ate - past tense of *eat*

For forty days Jesus was seen by many people.

forty - 40

was seen - past participle of *see*

They believed he really was the Promised Deliverer.

Then as the disciples were with Jesus one day he rose into the air and disappeared into heaven.

rose - past tense of *rise;* to go up

disappeared - past tense of *disappear.* go out of sight

heaven - up in the sky, a spiritual place of great beauty

Two angels came and told the men that Jesus would come back to earth again someday.

angels - spiritual beings that appear as men

Discussion Questions:
1. What happened that evening?
2. What did Jesus do?
3. What happened over the next 40 days?
4. What happened one day?
5. What did the angels say?
6. Do you think Jesus really will come back to earth some day?

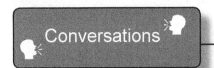 **Conversations**

Part 2

Thanksgiving:

Thanksgiving is an American harvest festival held in November. The Pilgrims and Indians thanked God for a good harvest. Today Americans have a big dinner and watch football games. Most countries have some kind of harvest festival.
What does your country do?

Grammar: verbs

	Present	Past
I you we they	thank decorate buy	thanked decorated bought
he she it	thanks decorates buys	thanked decorated bought

Christmas:

December 25 is the celebration of Jesus' birthday. People decorate their houses with Christmas trees, lights, and ornaments hanging on the branches. At the top of the tree is a star to remind people of the star of Bethlehem. People buy gifts for each other to remember the greatest gift ever given to humanity, Jesus.
There are special Christmas programs in many of the churches and on Christmas Day people have a family feast as families come together to celebrate.
There is also a tradition in many countries that on the night before Christmas a man named Santa Claus comes down the chimney and leaves presents for the children.
Do you celebrate Christmas in your country? What special things do you do?

Thanksgiving words:

harvest festival - crops are brought in
   give thanks to God - say thank you
Pilgrims - the first people from Europe
   to come and live in America
Indians- the people who were living in
   America
football games - teams play football
   on TV

Christmas words:

Jesus' birthday - celebrated
   December 25
decorate - put special things
   around the house
Christmas tree - symbol of
   Tree of Life
lights - lights of different
   colors
ornaments - things to hang
   on the tree
gifts - presents
humanity - people
Christmas programs - special
   church services
traditions - things people do
   every year
Santa Claus - represents
   St.Nicholas who gave
   presents to children
chimney - fireplace

15

Plans

Jesus' Return

Part 1

Discussion Questions:

Personal

Spiritual
Who is God?
Who is Jesus?
Character
What traits are important?
How can you improve your character?
Family / Friends
How do you act with your family/friends?
How can you treat them better?
Health
What can you do to have better health?
Education
Do you want to get more education?
What do you have to do?
Job
Do you like your job?
How can you make it better?

Family

Spiritual training
How can I help my family learn about God?
Character training
How can we (parents) help our children learn to have good values?
Marriage Partner
What can I do to make my marriage better?
Financial responsibilities
How can I make money for my family?
Health care
What can I do to keep my family healthy?
Fun
What can we do for fun?

Definitions:
goals - what you would like to have
character - what you believe and how you act
plans - what you hope to do
responsibility - what you have to do
appointments - scheduled meetings
recreation - things you do, usually outside
entertainment - things you do, usually inside
vacation - time away from work
reservations - to set aside for later use

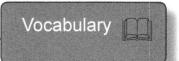

Goals

Personal
- spiritual
- character
- family
- friends
- health
- educational
- job

Family
- spiritual training
- character training
- marriage partner
- financial responsibilities
- health care
- fun

Plans are important if you want to be successful. You make plans to reach your goals. You can do almost anything that you decide you really want to do. Your character is the thing that helps you reach your goals. If you have a good character you will be happy.

Planning
calendars, planners
- Get a personal calendar or planner and write down appointments and meetings.
- Get a family calender or planner to keep track of appointments and responsibilites for all family members. Put the calendar in a place where it can be checked easily by all family members.

Recreation
camping, fishing, skiing, swimming, hiking, ball games, sports, vacations
- Planning for recreation is half of the fun.
- Plan for vacations or trips.
- Make lists of everything you are going to need.
- Then before you go check your list to make sure you have everything.
- Keep the list in a handy place so you can add to it when you think of something you are going to need.
- Often you will have to make reservations. You may need to purchase tickets for your planned activity.
- Make sure you take copies of reservation numbers and phone numbers that you may need.

Entertainment
movies, games, shopping, going out to eat, having coffee, hobbies
- These things don't involve as much planning.
- If you are meeting someone, make sure everyone clearly understands the time and place.

ex
exit
except
excuse
exchange
*****ex**plain
*****ex**tremely
*****ex**tinguisher

-al
person**al**
spiritu**al**
education**al**
financi**al**
recreation**al**
*****festiv**al**
*****tradition**al**
*****physic**al**
*****speci**al**
*****etern**al**

-ble
a**ble**
doa**ble**
worka**ble**
vlslb**le**
possi**ble**
*****valua**ble**
*****sensi**ble**
*****responsi**ble**
*****availa**ble**

all (al)
b**all**
footb**all**
m**all**
c**all**ed
t**all**
*****f**all**
*****alt**ogether**
*****al**ways
*****al**so

ə **(swah)**
about
amazed
pers**o**nal
every**o**ne
*****s**o**mething
*****cust**o**m
*****pres**e**nt
*****tr**a**dition

oi (oy)
app**oi**ntment
enj**oy**
ann**oy**
t**oy**s
s**oy**
oil
*****s**oi**l
*****j**oi**n
*****t**oi**let
*****c**oi**ns

Rhythm

to**geth**er
go **shop**ping
have **cof**fee
ap**point**ment
*****dis**ci**ples
*****wher**ev**er
*****be**liev**ers

fi**nan**cial
va**ca**tion
the **fu**ture
*****the **week**end
*****the **judge**ment
*****for**ev**er
*****He's **com**ing

 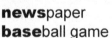

newspaper
baseball game
*****meet**ing place
*****char**acter
*****every**one
*****Sat**urday

***** Asterisks indicate Part 2 words.

IDIOMS

● ● ● ●

Don't spread yourself too thin.
* Don't try to do too much work
She was very tired. She _spread herself too thin_.

● ● ●

Make ends meet.
* To budget your money so it
  will pay all of your bills
I just paid my taxes, and
I am _making ends meet_.

● ●

Look forward to
* to plan something that is fun
I _look forward to_ our vacation.

● ●

Put your money where your mouth is.
* Invest in something you believe in
If you think it is a good deal, you need to
put your money where your mouth is.

● ●

Pay through the nose
* Pay too much money
If you have to go to professional football game,
you will have to _pay through the nose._

Bible
Lesson

Part 1

God's Plan

**After Jesus went up to heaven, the disciples told everyone about the
Deliverer wherever they went.**
Many people became believers.
Believers met together to learn God's Word, worship, and pray.
These groups became churches.
God used some church leaders to write the rest of the Bible.

Discussion Questions:
1. Where did Jesus go?
2. What did the disciples tell about wherever they went?
3. Did many people believe them?
4. When believers met what did they do?
5. What is a church?
6. How did we get the rest of the Bible?

Grammar: verbs

	Present	Past
I you we they	go pray use	went prayed used
he she it	goes prays uses	went prayed used

Part 2

The good news about Jesus spread to many countries.
Today there are many churches all over the world.
When Jesus left the earth He promised to return some day.
Then He will come to rule as King of the earth.
Jesus will defeat Satan in a final battle.
Everyone will stand before God.
Those who have believed in Jesus, the Deliverer, will live
**   with God forever.**
Those who have not believed in Jesus, the Deliverer, will be
**   punished forever for their own sins.**

Discussion Questions:

1. How far did the good news spread?
2. What did Jesus promise?
3. What will happen to Satan?
4. What will <u>everyone</u> have to do?
5. What happens to believers?
6. What happens to those who don't believe?
7. Describe the new heaven and earth.

Jesus has gone to prepare us a place for believers.
 - Matt 24, Mark 13, II Timothy3:1-4
Jesus will return for believers.
 - John 14, Revelation

Grammar: verbs

	<u>Present</u>	<u>Past</u>
I	spread	spread
you	defeat	defeated
we	stand	stood
they	punish	punished
he	spreads	spread
she	defeats	defeated
it	stands	stood
	punishes	punished

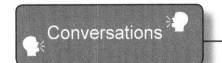

Part 2

Past - Present - Future

Discuss the concept of time.

What kind of work have you done in the past?
Where have you lived?
What were your dreams when you were young?

What kind of work are you doing now?
Where do you live now?
What are your dreams now?

What kind of work do you want to do in the future?
Where do you want to live?
What plans do you have to reach your dreams?

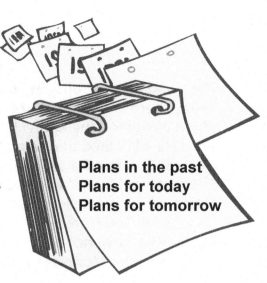

Plans in the past
Plans for today
Plans for tomorrow

Discussions:
What are your plans for today?
Do you have any appointments?
How would you like to ____?
Let's get together and ____.

What are your plans for the weekend?
Are you free <u>Saturday</u>?
Would you like to ___?

What are your plans for the future?
Are you going to look for a job?
What kind of job are you looking for?
Are you going to <u>college</u>?
What are you going to do <u>when you finish school</u>?
Are you planning <u>a vacation</u>?
Where would you like to go?
How much time do you have for <u>a vacation</u>?
How much will it cost?

Spending spree
* To spend a lot of money
She went on a <u>spending spree</u>.

Throwing away your money
* Spending your money foolishly
Don't <u>throw your money away</u>.

Personal Planning

Write down some dreams / goals that you have for yourself.
What plans do you have to reach those goals?
What are your goals for the next 5 years? 10 years?
What would you have to do to have your dreams come true?
How long would it take for you to reach those goals?
How much would it cost?
What are some of your duties now that may or may not get in the way of your goals?
Are you willing to do the work and probably the sacrifice that it takes to get to your
    dreams?

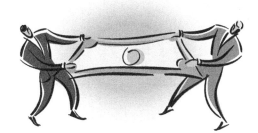

Financial planning:

Do you have a plan?

*Now - How much money do you have?
*Future - How much do you want to have?
           How are you going to reach your goals?

● ●

Stretching the dollar
* Spending your money wisely
It is hard to <u>stretch our dollars.</u>

Make a Budget based on the plan.
   1. Gather every financial statement you have.
   2. Write down how much you make each month.
   3. Make a list of monthly expenses.
   4. Break expenses in two parts:

Needs	_Wants_
food	car
housing	toys
utilities	telephone
electricity	cell phone
water	computer
trash	television
clothes	

   5. Total your monthly income and monthly expenses.
   6. Make adjustments to expenses.
   7. Review your budget monthly.

Balance your budget.

161

Christian Beliefs

1. God loves you and wants to give you eternal life.

    John 3:16 - "For God so loved the world that He gave His only son that whoever believes in Him will not die, but will have everlasting life."

    Romans 6:23b - "... the gift of God is eternal life through Jesus Christ our Lord."

2. We are separated from God because we are sinful.

    Romans 3:23 - "For all have sinned and fall short of the glory of God."

    Romans 6:23b "...the wages of sin is death."

3. Jesus took our punishment for our sins on the CROSS. When He rose from the dead He showed us that He conquered death.

    Romans 5:8 - "But God demonstrates His own love for us in this: While we were still sinners, Christ died for us."

    John 5:24 - Jesus said,"I tell you the truth, whoever hears my word and believes Him (God) who sent me has eternal life and will not be condemned; he has crossed over from death to life."

4. Ask Jesus to forgive your sin and turn your life over to Jesus to lead you for the rest of your life.

    Acts 10:43 - "All the prophets testify about Him (Jesus) that every one who believes in Him receives forgiveness of sin through His name."

    John 1:12 - "Yet to all who received Him, to those who believed in His name, He gave the right to become children of God."

Extra Idioms

Knock someone's socks off
* To really impress someone

Stretching the dollar
* Spending your money wisely

Throwing away your money
* Spending your money foolishly

Spending spree
* To spend a lot of money

163

BASIC GRAMMAR

Nouns - persons, places, things (including animals)
Pronouns - I, he, she, it, you, we, they
Verbs - action and being
Adjectives - describe nouns
Adverbs - describe adjectives or other adverbs
Conjunctions - connecting words
Prepositions - a relation or function word

Nouns

People	Places	Things
mother	garden	trees
father	house	birds
son	restaurant	world
daughter	store	heavens

Pronouns
I, he, she, it, you (singular and plural), we, they
Possessive Pronouns
me, my, mine, your, his, her, our, their

Verbs
Tenses

Present - happening now
Past - happening before
Future - happening later

Present Progressive - present linking verb + meaning verb with <u>ing</u>
Past Progressive - past linking verb + meaning verb with <u>ing</u>
Future Progressive- will + linking verb + meaning verb with <u>ing</u>

Present Perfect - have / has + past tense verb
Past Perfect - had + past tense verb
Future Perfect - will have / has + past tense verb

Present	Past	Future
am / is / are	was / were	will be
Present Progressive	**Past Progressive**	**Future Progressive**
am / is /are going	was / were going	will be going
Present Perfect	**Past Perfect**	**Future Perfect**
have / has been	had been	will have been

Examples: Verb - to be

Present tense
I <u>am</u> a mother.
He <u>is</u> a father.
She <u>is</u> a sister.
It <u>is</u> a dog.
You <u>are</u> a brother.
You (all) <u>are</u> cousins.
We <u>are</u> a family.
They <u>are</u> cousins.

Past tense
I <u>was</u> happy.
He <u>was</u> sad.
She <u>was</u> mad.
It <u>was</u> cold.
You <u>were</u> fine.
You (all) <u>were</u> happy.
We <u>were</u> okay.
They <u>were</u> nice.

Future tense
I <u>will be</u> home.
He <u>will be</u> 2 next month.
She <u>will be</u> 30 in June.
It <u>will be</u> 5 o'clock.
You <u>will be</u> seven.
You (all) <u>will be</u> at school.
We <u>will be</u> at church.
They <u>will be</u> here soon.

Present Progressive
I am going to the store.
He is going to school.
She is going to work.
It is going to rain.
You are going with me.
We are going on a trip.
They are going to bed.

Past Progressive
I was going to call.
He was going with you.
She was going home
It was going to snow.
You were going outside.
We were going to a show.
They were going, too.

Future Progressive
I will be going at 3 o'clock.
He will be going at 4 o'clock.
She will be going at 5 o'clock.
It will be going out on Friday.
You will be going home soon.
We will be going to to work.
They will be going with us.

Present Perfect
I have been working.
He has been working.
She has been working.
You have been working.
We have been working.
They have been working.

Past Perfect
I had been there before.
(all pronouns are the same)

Future Perfect
I will have been at this job
for a month on June 4.
(all pronouns are the same)

Made in the USA
Coppell, TX
08 July 2022

79668505R00092